738.1 Woo

D1589068

3 8022 0 043992 7

HANDBUILDING CERAMIC FORMS

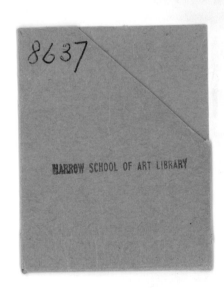

8637

HARROW SCHOOL OF ART LIBRARY

Also by Elsbeth S. Woody
POTTERY ON THE WHEEL
(with photographs by Steven Smolker)

ELSBETH S. WOODY

HANDBUILDING CERAMIC FORMS

JOHN MURRAY

First published in Great Britain 1979
by John Murray (Publishers) Ltd.,
50 Albemarle Street, London W1X 4BD
Copyright © 1978 by Elsbeth S. Woody
Photographs 245–56 by Penny Hood Hoagland
All other photographs, except where noted otherwise,
by Elsbeth S. Woody
All rights reserved
Designed by Jacqueline Schuman
Printed in Great Britain by
J. W. Arrowsmith Ltd., Bristol

British Library Cataloguing in Publication Data

Woody, Elsbeth Siglinde
    Handbuilding ceramic forms.
    1. Pottery craft
    I. Title
    738.1   TT920

ISBN 0-7195-3653-7

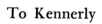

To Kennerly

Acknowledgments

Many people have been involved in the preparation of this book. My deepest appreciation goes to the artists, who have both given freely of their time and shared with me their knowledge and feelings about their work. I not only learned a great deal about ceramics from them but also have found new friends.

Equally important to this book was Penny Hood Hoagland, whose hands appear in the photographs throughout the first part of the book. Her patience was unending and her experience as a potter invaluable.

My thanks also go to Tom and Madeline Lewis, both for starting my writing career and for their continuous encouragement and help.

To my friend and colleague, Professor Virginia Smith, I am grateful for advice on many matters concerning this book.

Julie Terestman will be fondly remembered for carrying dozens of rolls of film back and forth to be processed.

To Pat Strachan my gratitude for guiding me once again through the complicated process of getting this book into print.

But most of all I feel indebted to my husband, Kennerly, not only for his help as editor but more importantly for his unending moral support. Without him I would not have dared to start, and without his help I would never have finished.

E.S.W.

Preface

Long before the invention of the potter's wheel, which occurred around 3000 B.C., man was forming vessels and sculptures out of clay by hand without the aid of a mechanical device. Many cultures today employ only handbuilding techniques and the contemporary craftsperson and ceramic sculptor have again turned their attention to those techniques. This is in large part due to the incredible variety of forms and expressions possible. Wheelthrown pottery is always round and symmetrical, at least initially, since it relies on the principle of rotation around a central axis. Handbuilt pottery, on the other hand, does not rely on any one principle of construction; a number of diverse methods are possible, each determining a certain look and feeling. Endless combinations and variations of technique—together with the fact that the clay can be worked at various consistencies, and the fact that limitation in size is dictated only by the size of the kiln or the weight of the pieces—make possible a very personal approach to the making of ceramic forms.

For the beginner two additional advantages may be important: first, only a small number of simple tools are needed, and, second, the skill of handling clay can be acquired quickly. Some of the most exciting works are based on very simple techniques. The novice, in other words, can almost from the onset concentrate on form and an intimate understanding of and feeling for clay, rather than on the acquisition of a technical skill, as is the case in learning the use of the potter's wheel.

The first part of the book will deal with the most basic information on the nature of clay, a discussion of the necessary tools, and a detailed explanation of the most common forming methods and surface treatments. The emphasis will be on the process of making ceramic forms and on the underlying principles, rather than on the making of specific works.

The second part will show how professionals are using those techniques, how they vary them and combine them to make works that range from the utilitarian to the most expressive and sculptural, as well as from the small-scale to the architectural.

E.S.W.

Contents

BASIC PROCESSES AND TECHNIQUES 1

8 | HANDBUILDING WITH WHEELTHROWN FORMS   133

TEN APPROACHES TO HANDBUILDING   139

BASIC PROCESSES AND TECHNIQUES

1

Technical Information on Clay

The Nature of Clay

Clay, one of the most abundant minerals, was formed from igneous rock through a geological weathering process that took place millions of years ago. By exposing clay to sufficiently high heat, we can turn it again into a rocklike, hard substance of enormous durability that is often impervious to water and even acids.

Since clay can be found almost anywhere—along rivers and lakes, and just below the topsoil—an enormous industry exists to mine, pulverize, test, and sell it. Objects made out of clay are part of our everyday lives and take forms that we may not be aware of. It is not only the craftsperson and artist who use clay; the major part of what is mined is used by industry for a variety of products from planters to bathroom fixtures.

In order to work with clay intelligently, it is essential to know at least some of its specific characteristics and the terminology associated with it.

Chemically, clay is hydrated aluminosilicate, which means that it contains alumina and silica, as well as chemically combined water. No clay, however, is that pure in its chemical composition. Clays vary a great deal, due to chemical variations among the parent rocks and also because the clay, when transported from its original site by wind, water, or glacier, picked up what might in a chemical sense be called impurities.

Under the microscope, the shape of the clay particle is flat and six-sided. These particles cling to each other at the same time as they slide on each other, provided sufficient water is in between the particles. The size of the particles can vary for several reasons. The weathering process may have progressed differently; the transportation of the clay may have resulted in sedimentation of different-size particles at different places; or the transportation may have ground some of the clays into finer particles.

What all this means to the potter is that there are many different clays at his disposal. They vary in color, particle size, and the temperature to which they can be fired. Some clays are white, others buff, red, or gray. This color range is due to the presence of different metals in the clay. Because of the various particle sizes, clays vary in texture, plasticity (the smaller the particle, the more plastic the clay), and the amount of shrinkage. In addition, clays mature at different temperatures: some clays may need a much higher temperature to become hard and durable than others.

Formulation of a Clay Body

The potter has to select a clay that fits his or her needs. Although not impossible, it is difficult to find a type of clay that fits your requirements without alterations. For this reason, most potters want a specific clay body; that is, a mixture of different types of clays and other minerals suitable to their needs as regards maturing point, color, texture shrinkage, and plasticity.

The formulation of a clay body is a science and should not be undertaken without a thorough understanding of the materials available or without a careful analysis of one's needs. Most potters arrive at a clay-body formula through a general knowledge of the types of clays available and through experimentation. The beginning potter should go to an experienced potter for help, rather than to a ceramic supply house. The clay bodies sold there are often formulated by ceramic engineers and are not necessarily the result of practical experience. A combination of the technical knowledge of the engineer and the practical experience of the potter is essential. Any clay-body formula should be thoroughly tested before you mix a large batch. The tests should include a shrinkage test, an absorption test (see D. Rhodes, *Clay and Glazes for the Potter*), and actual use under the same conditions in which the clay will be used. A clay-body formula is a highly personal thing, and what is perfect for one potter might not suit another.

Clay bodies can be mixed by the potter or they can be purchased premixed. Commercial ceramic supply houses mix and sell clay bodies, which can be purchased in any amounts, from ten pounds to a ton or more. Buying small amounts of clay is expensive. Since clay improves with age (aging increases the plasticity of the clay) and since it can be kept moist for months if it is properly covered, you should buy more than you immediately need. Commercial outfits will mix clay according to your own specifications, but it is almost always necessary in such cases to buy large amounts.

Common Terminology

All clays share a common terminology. The terms *slip, plastic, leather-hard,* and *bone-dry* refer to clay with various amounts of water in it. Slip is clay at a mayonnaise consistency and, as we shall see, is most often used as a kind of glue between two pieces of clay or as a means to decorate the ceramic piece with a different-colored clay.

Clay is worked on most often at the plastic stage; that is, when the clay is wet enough to have maximum plasticity (a coil should bend without cracking), but not so wet that it sticks to your hands or tools. Leather-hard refers to a stage where clay has been allowed to dry somewhat but still contains moisture. It can be dented and slightly bent.

Clay is bone-dry when it has been allowed to dry completely. Very rarely is a piece worked on at this stage.

The water that evaporates when the clay has been allowed to dry is called the *water of plasticity.* It is the water between the particles. This water of plasticity can be returned into the clay over and over again.

Greenware refers to all unfired ceramic ware.

Stages of Firing

Once the piece of ceramic has been allowed to dry completely, it can be placed in the kiln and fired.

When exposed to heat, all clays change radically, both in physical form and in chemical composition. They go through various stages, the most important of which are the expulsion of the atmospheric moisture at 212° Fahrenheit and the expulsion of the chemically combined water at 600° Fahrenheit. The expulsion of the chemically combined water is the first major chemical change and is irreversible. Quartz conversion, a change in the silica crystals, and the change of all clay components into oxide form occur by the time the pot reaches the stage of *vitrification,* the final step in firing. Vitrification means that certain components of the clay melt and form a crystalline structure within the clay. This causes the hardness and durability of the fired clay. If carried to completion, vitrification would result in the complete melting of the ceramic piece.

A clay body is mature when vitrification has taken place to the extent that the clay is hard and durable and, in the case of stoneware and porcelain, impervious to water and acid. As we have said, clays mature at different temperatures, and it is essential to determine the maturing point when you acquire your clay.

Firing Schedules

Firing schedules have to take the above stages into account. The atmospheric moisture and chemically combined water are driven off in the form of steam. Because of the force of steam and the danger of an explosion that would burst the pot, you must proceed slowly with the firing at this point. Depending on the complexity of the shape and the thickness of the ware, as well as the denseness of the clay body, three to five hours should be allowed for the piece to reach 1000° Fahrenheit. Very thick sculptural pieces are fired even more slowly at this initial stage. At the time of oxidation of all components, at 1600° Fahrenheit, it is essential that enough oxygen be present in the kiln. Vitrification should also be allowed to proceed slowly and evenly throughout the kiln, since shrinkage occurs at this stage. Depending on the type of ware that is fired, the kind of clay body used, and the temperature one fires to, firings take from six to twenty-four hours. After the desired temperature is reached, all holes in the kiln are closed to slow down the cooling of the kiln. As a rule of thumb, the cooling period should be at least as long as the firing period. The pieces should not be removed from the kiln until they can be touched with bare hands.

A distinction is made between bisque and glaze firing. If the ware is to be glazed, most potters bisque-fire their ware, which means they fire to a point just before vitrification sets in. This way the ware is still absorbent but also strong enough to be handled in glazing. After glazing, the ware is fired to the proper vitrification temperature of the clay and glaze.

Glazes

A glaze is defined by Daniel Rhodes in *Clay and Glazes for the Potter* as a "glassy coating melted in place on a ceramic body." This glassy coating consists of a compound of minerals that have been ground to a fine powder, carefully weighed out according to a glaze recipe, mixed with water, applied to the pot, and then fused to it by heat. Glazing, thus, involves the formulation of a glaze recipe, mixing it, applying it, and firing. The most complex of these is the formulation of the glaze recipe. Potters arrive at glaze formulas either by a thorough knowledge of the glaze materials and a great deal of experimentation, or they borrow from books, friends, or magazines. A glaze recipe always has to be thoroughly tested and often modified to fit one's particular needs. It is also imperative to know the firing range of a glaze, since it can be extremely narrow. A glaze that is beautiful at 2250° may run off the pot at 2280°. Application of a glaze varies from pot to pot, but falls generally into four categories: the pot can be dipped into the glaze, the glaze can be poured over the pot, it can be brushed, or it can be sprayed on. Although glazes can be applied to greenware, most potters bisque-fire their pieces first. Glazes can be shiny or matte, transparent or opaque, with numerous colors. Special glazing effects, such as fuming, lustering, salt glazing, rakuing, etc., further enlarge the repertoire of ceramic finishes.

Classification According to Temperature Fired

All fired ceramic ware can be classified according to the temperature at which the clay matures. *Earthenware* refers to all ceramic forms fired to about 1800°; *stoneware* is fired to about 2300°; *porcelain* is white translucent ware that has been fired in excess of 2300°. Each of these requires a different clay body and glaze.

These different types of wares differ greatly in appearance as well as in hardness and strength. Earthenware pottery is usually still water absor-

bent, and the glazes tend to be, although they do not have to be, brightly colored and shiny. Stoneware is usually impervious to water and acids and it is much stronger than earthenware. The colors of the glazes are much more muted, but the bond between the glaze and the clay is stronger, which means the glaze is less likely to chip off. Porcelain always refers to a white clay that is highly vitrified and in the most refined cases takes on a kind of translucence.

Common Characteristics of Clay: The Maxims

Even though there are a number of different clays, they share four unique characteristics, though to different degrees. These characteristics are extremely important, since almost all rules that govern how one works with clay can be deduced from them. They are the "maxims" of ceramics.

One, *clay is plastic when sufficiently wet*. It can be pushed and stretched without losing its cohesion, as wet sand would. This is due to the flatness of the particles. As I said before, the particles cling to each other, but also slide on each other, very much like panes of glass that have water between them. The amount of plasticity is determined by the particle size (the smaller the particle, the more plastic the clay), the amount of carbonaceous material in the clay (which increases with aging), the surface tension of the water (the colder and harder the water, the more plastic the clay), and even the electrical charge of certain types of clay particles.

Two, *clay shrinks as it dries and when it vitrifies*. This fact should always be in the back of the ceramicist's mind. Clay shrinks first when the water of plasticity evaporates and the particles draw closer together. This means that the shrinkage (like the plasticity) depends on the particle size and the amount of water present. Clay shrinks again during vitrification, since certain components in the clay melt, tightening the structure.

The consequences of shrinkage are many and highly important to the handbuilder. Frequent reference will be made to this property in discussing the various techniques. The necessary precautions that have to be taken are, however, largely a matter of common sense. For instance: clays of vastly different water content, physical makeup, and type cannot be joined. Clay walls of different thicknesses shrink at different rates and this may cause cracking. Non-shrinking materials cannot be used as supports, and if non-shrinking materials like grog or fiberglass, sand, etc., are added to the clay, they have to be of a relatively small particle size. In drying and firing, provisions must be made for the movement of the clay during shrinkage. For instance, the bottom of a pot should not stick to the board or shelf. A layer of grog or a piece of cloth is put underneath very large pieces to facilitate the movement. Forms that touch the board or shelf in more than one area should be put on top of a clay slab that shrinks at the same rate. This alleviates the stress on the form.

Three, *clay hardens at its dries*. Plastic clay is totally lacking in structural strength. Forms made with plastic clay are extremely susceptible to distortions and have to be handled with great care. As the clay dries, it becomes harder and stronger. Leather-hard clay supports its own weight very well—it neither sags nor tears—and by the time it is bone-dry, it is as hard as wood. On the other hand, bone-dry clay is very brittle, and forms at this stage also have to be handled with care. The fact that clay hardens as it dries is continuously exploited by the ceramicist and in particular the handbuilder. Large forms or forms that project outward or forms with suddenly changing profiles can be built in steps. The lower part is allowed to dry and harden somewhat before more weight is put on top, in order to prevent it from sagging. Refinement of form can take place at the leather-hard stage because of the increased strength of the clay. The harder the clay gets, however, the less plastic it is.

Four, *clay vitrifies when subjected to sufficient heat*. Clay becomes hard and durable and, in the case of stoneware and porcelain, impervious to water and acids when subjected to sufficient heat. The transformation is total and the pot is virtually reborn in the firing.

For more complete discussions of the nature of clay and particularly of the technology and techniques of glazing and firing, refer to the works cited in the Bibliographical Note. The emphasis in this book is on forming techniques. Only those aspects of the technology of clay that are important to them have been discussed.

2

Tools and Working Space

1

One of the advantages of working with hand-building techniques is that only a small number of very simple tools are needed for the forming of the pieces [1].* Almost all these tools are part of any household.

A piece of ¾-inch marine plywood, covered with heavy canvas or even just an old bedsheet stretched tightly over it or glued to it, will suffice as a working surface. It should be placed on a sturdy table, so that clay can be beaten out on it. A few pieces of marine plywood of various sizes to build the pieces on, several flat pieces of cloth, a dull knife, a fork, a brush, a length of twisted wire (thin picture-frame wire) with buttons as ends, are all you need to get started.

To keep clay moist, pieces of thin plastic, the type you get at the dry cleaner's, are essential.

---
* Numbers in brackets refer to photographs.

For clean-up tools, a scraper, a terry-cloth towel, and a sponge will do.

Some techniques demand specific tools, such as rolling pins, wooden dowels, or cheesecloth. Flexible metal ribs, wooden ribs, and modeling tools come in handy with almost any technique, and these are ceramic tools that are usually available only in ceramic supply houses. The metal ribs come in a variety of oval or crescent shapes, with either smooth or serrated edges. They are useful in scraping the surface of clay. The modeling tools are made of wood, are thin and elongated, and also come in a great variety of shapes and sizes. Their functions can vary widely —from texturing the clay to smoothing it, for example, or serving as extensions of the fingers where the fingers cannot reach. A turntable is convenient, yet not absolutely necessary. I worked for years without one, yet became addicted to it as soon as I had one.

The tools that I cannot get along without are paddles. They are made out of wood (so that clay does not stick to them) and should have some weight. I have a variety of shapes—some flat with the edges sanded, some rounded, each one doing a particular job. Some ceramic supply houses now carry them, but mine are all made or adapted from other uses, such as half a child's baseball bat, wooden spoons, darning knobs, etc. They are used in shaping, surface treatment, and joining.

For more complex work, additional tools such as levels or dollies, might become necessary. And of course every ceramicist has his or her own particular indispensable tool, most of which would never be found in an art supply house.

Almost any space can be converted into a small ceramic shop. I have seen people work in family rooms or kitchens, but a garage or basement will serve much better. Even though handbuilding is less messy than wheelthrowing, dust can be a problem. There should be enough space to work comfortably in, with room for shelves, the containers for clay and clay scraps, as well as a slab of plaster about four inches thick on which to dry and wedge the clay. A sink is handy, but not mandatory. In the winter the area should be kept warm. Wet pots will freeze when the temperature drops below freezing and collapse when they thaw. Chunks of clay that freeze and defrost are usually very wet on the outside, with a hard inner core.

Making the forms is only one step in the total process. Glazing and firing facilities are required to finish the product.

Your needs will change with time and will vary with the kind of work you are doing. Ceramic shops where small-scale production work is done have to be laid out differently than those meant to accommodate architectural and large sculptural pieces. Each ceramicist must arrive at a suitable physical setup mostly through trial and error.

3
Preparation of Clay

Mixing and Reprocessing

As emphasized earlier, it is essential to find a clay body suitable to your needs. Clay can be purchased premixed to the proper consistency (and in some cases even de-aired) or you can mix it youself by carefully weighing out the ingredients, mixing them, and adding the mixture to water. Most clay bodies need 25 to 30 percent of their dry weight in water, but when mixing in this manner, add the dry clay materials to at least 40 percent of their weight in water. After sitting overnight, the clay can then be dried on a plaster slab to the proper working consistency (see p. 94 ff. on making plaster forms). Mixing clay in this manner is a laborious and dusty process. If large amounts of clay are needed, the acquisition of a clay mixer, or the purchase of premixed clay, may be necessary.

It is also important to realize that freshly mixed clay is usually quite short; that is, it lacks plasticity. Therefore, it is necessary to allow the clay to sit at least a week before using it. The longer the clay is stored at the plastic stage, the more plastic it becomes.

Clay that has become too hard to work with can be dealt with in two ways. If it is just a little too hard, I simply wrap it with a soaking-wet towel and plastic and let the whole package sit overnight. The clay usually absorbs enough moisture from the towel to be workable.

Another way is to let the clay dry completely and then soak it in water until it disintegrates, which happens faster in a low, wide tub than in a deep garbage can. The clay is then pulled out and left on a plaster slab to dry to the proper consistency. Occasional turning allows the clay to dry out more evenly. If you leave spaces between small mounds of clay, it will dry out faster.

2

Wedging

No matter in what manner the clay is prepared, wedging it becomes unavoidable. The purpose of wedging is to make the ball of clay perfectly homogeneous. In other words, it mixes all materials evenly, including the water, and removes all air bubbles.

Wedging can be done in a number of ways. For the beginner, simple *handwedging* is enough. A handful of clay is twisted apart and pushed together again until the clay feels even in terms of water content [2].

Spiral wedging is the professional and most efficient way to wedge. This kind of wedging consists of two interlocking motions. The left hand rotates and guides the clay, while the right hand does the kneading. These motions are done rapidly and from forty to one hundred times, depending on the condition of the clay. This technique is hard to learn but far superior to any of the others. In order to understand the position of the hands, one must start with the final product of spiral wedging—a cone standing on its point [3]. The left hand is placed, slightly cupped, over the base of the cone and remains there throughout the wedging procedure, while the right hand is placed on the side but along the edge of the base.

With each sequence of interlocking motions between the left and right hand, the cone is rotated on its point.

3

To begin, push the clay into a rough cone shape and lay it on its side with the point toward you. Place the left hand, slightly cupped, over the base [4]. Lift the cone up on its point in a spiral, clockwise motions with that left hand [5]. Place the right hand at the side of the cone with the thumb and index finger along the edge of the base of the cone [6]. Swivel the left hand counter-clockwise one-quarter turn without releasing the clay [7], and press down with the

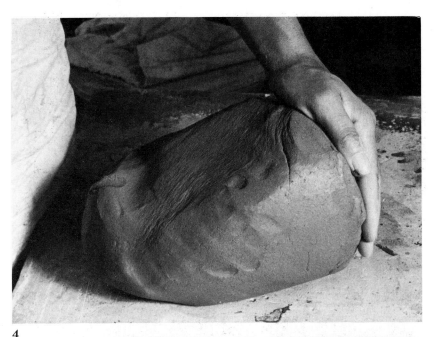

4

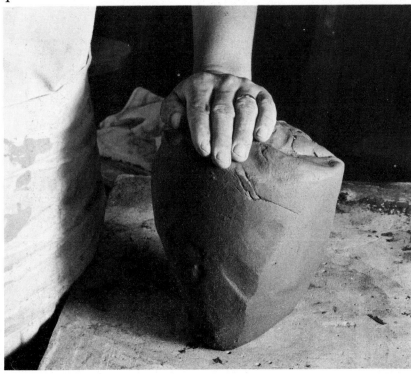

5

6

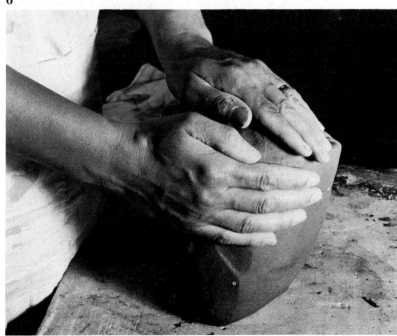

7

8   9

heel of the right hand, folding some clay down from behind [8, 9]. The left hand remains on the clay but does not exert any pressure. The left hand is then in a position to lift the clay in a clockwise spiral [10]; the right hand goes behind the previous indentation of the heel of the hand on the side of the cone, but along that edge of the base; swivel the left hand, press down and so on.

The clay should assume a tongue-like shape [10] with a clear pattern of folds, a sharp indentation from the heel of the right hand, and a slight indentation from the left hand. The two

hands have totally different functions and actions. The left hand rotates the clay, lifts it into the right hand, and guides it, while the right hand presses the clay down. The clay is rotated only while it is lifted. It is pressed down straight, without rotation.

It is important to realize that wedging is done not only with the hands but with the entire body. Your feet should be planted firmly so you can rock back and forth, using the weight of your body when pressing down.

The surface on which you wedge should be lower than a normal table, at about the height

10

of your wrist, and slightly absorbent. For clay of
the proper consistency, wedge on wood or hard
asbestos board; for wet clay, use a slab of plaster.
It is difficult to tell when the clay is sufficiently
wedged—the wedging time is entirely determined by the condition of the clay. When the
clay feels dense and tightly structured, it has
been sufficiently wedged. Start to press down less
and less with the heel of the right hand, while
still going through the other motions. This will
produce the cone shape. The base of the cone can
be rocked on the slab to produce a smooth convex surface.

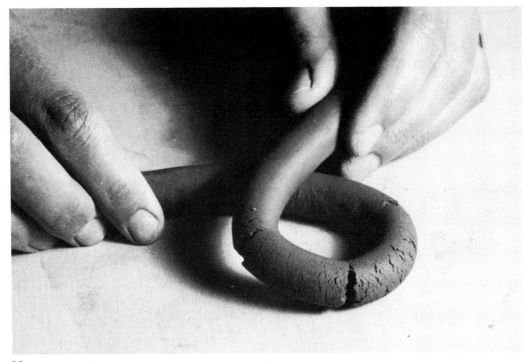

11

Working Consistency of Clay

The proper working consistency is hard to describe. We usually work the clay at the plastic stage. Plastic, however, is a relative term. In general if the clay does not stick to your hands and if a coil can be bent without developing large cracks [11] it is the proper consistency for most techniques. (Small surface cracks can be ignored.) It should be pointed out that different techniques demand different consistencies of clay and also that ceramicists often have personal preferences.

4

Considerations Common to All Forming Methods

Before going into the detailed description of the various handbuilding methods, I would like to discuss certain aspects that all these techniques have in common. They are directly related to the consequences of the shrinkage of the clay, and the fact that clay hardens as it dries. In addition, it is important to point out that all these techniques are based on the assumption that when one thinks of ceramic forms one almost always thinks in terms of hollow forms. This is necessitated not only by the weight of clay but also by the fact that moisture can easily be trapped inside solid masses of clay, causing the piece to explode during firing. If the piece demands that you work with a solid mass, even the smallest form should be pierced to allow the moisture to escape.

Joining

No matter how one works with clay, one eventually has to join two pieces of clay together. Proper joining methods are extremely important because of the stresses exerted on the joint by the shrinkage of the clay in the drying and firing.

To go into every possible joining situation would be very complicated and confusing. I shall therefore limit the following discussion to general principles which should be taken into consideration in all situations: (1) the types of joints possible; (2) the consistency of the clay to be joined; and (3) other factors and techniques, such as contact area, paddling, and timing, that apply to every type of joint.

12

13

Types of Joints: Butt and Overlap

To insure a secure bond between two pieces, clay from one piece should be moved over to the other piece. This can be done quite easily in the case of an overlap joint [12]. But in the case of a butt joint—that is, when the ends meet without overlapping—smearing clay from one side of the joint to the other is not always possible without weakening one side. In this case, a coil can be added over the joint [13]. This coil adheres to both sides and provides a secure bond between them.

Overlap joints in general are stronger than butt joints. However, if the reinforcing coil is pushed firmly into the joint, a butt joint can withstand considerable stress. When placing the coil, push it firmly into the joint with the index finger moving along the seam in small steps [13]. Counteract this pressure by supporting the clay on the other side with your hand.

A butt joint occurs whenever two ends meet, rather than overlap, and also whenever an end butts onto a side, as in the case of a box shape, or when the side stands on a bottom [14].

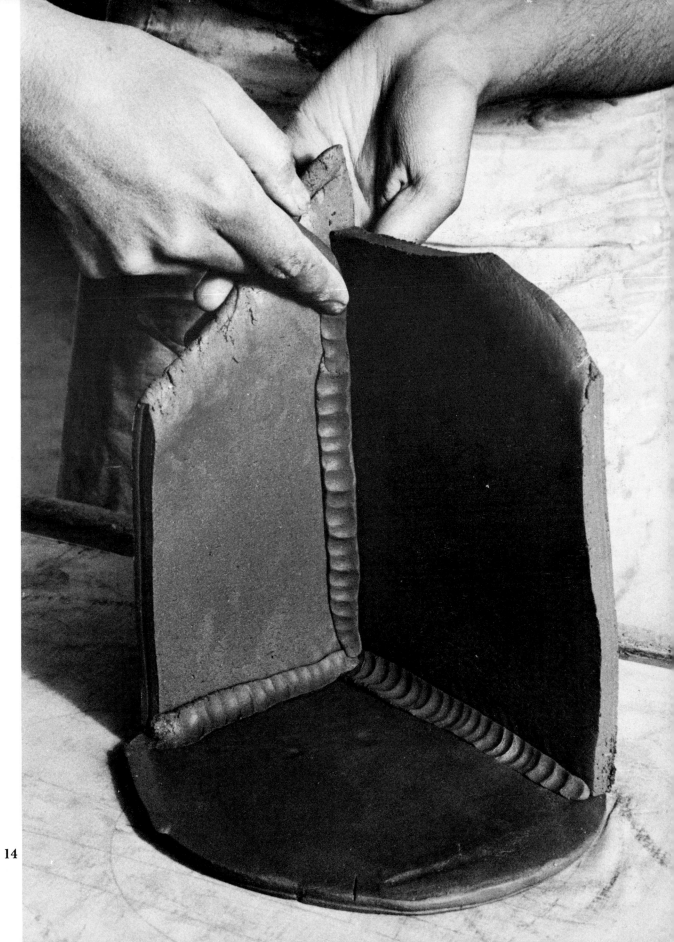

14

Consistency of Clay to Be Joined

Because clay shrinks as it dries, one has to be aware of the water content of the pieces of clay that one joins.

When one is joining *plastic* to *plastic* clay, it is usually not necessary to use water or any other bond, since pieces of plastic clay adhere to each other quite easily.

However, if one joins *plastic* clay to *leather-hard* clay, or *leather-hard* to *leather-hard,* the special precaution of scoring and slipping has to take place. In the area of contact between the two pieces of clay, the leather-hard clay is scored or scratched with a fork, knife, or comb at right angles to the seam, and slip, or water, is brushed on it [15].

The scoring does two things: (1) it allows the water to penetrate and (2) enables the joining clay to grip the scored clay better for a much tighter bond.

"Scoring and slipping" should be done *wherever* plastic clay touches leather-hard, and also *wherever* leather-hard is to be joined to leather-hard. In the latter case, both pieces have to be scored and at least one slipped. This procedure of scoring and slipping applies to both the butt and overlap joints, and also to the areas where a joint is reinforced with plastic clay [16].

Sometimes, however, I make exceptions to the "wherever" rule: I try to avoid scoring and slipping when it may disturb the look of the piece. In the case of a butt joint when the slip may seep out and disturb the pattern, for example, I score and slip only on the inside, where the reinforcing clay touches the leather-hard clay.

For an overlap joint, I may score and slip only part of the overlap, to prevent the slip from oozing out.

Whenever I break the rule, however, I am fully aware of the chances I am taking.

I also make an exception to the "no water" rule in joining plastic to plastic clay: when I am adding small pieces of plastic clay to a larger

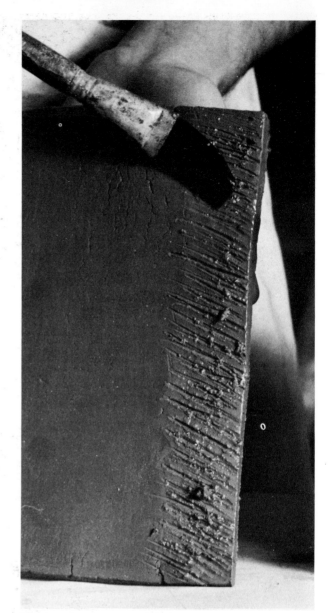

15

piece of plastic clay, I dampen the small pieces for a better bond [17].

The rules of joining, then, are quite simple. Reinforce a butt joint, smear clay from one side to the other in an overlap joint. Score and slip the leather-hard clay wherever plastic clay touches the leather-hard and when leather-hard is joined to leather-hard clay.

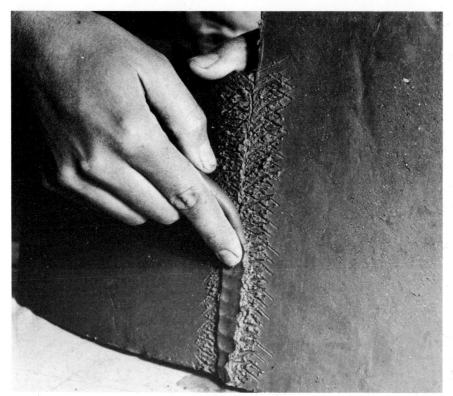

16

17

18

Common Factors in Joining

In addition to these simple rules, there are considerations that are common to all joining procedures. The most important ones relate to the size of the contact area between the two pieces to be joined.

Whereas metal can be held together by a few spot-welds, this is not possible with clay. The larger the contact area, the better. To maximize the contact, there are a number of procedures that can be followed: (1) Secure the entire seam, not just sections of it. (2) Cut the edges of slabs at an angle before joining, particularly when they are leather-hard [18]; this increases the contact area enormously. (3) Embed the reinforcing coil into a groove that is made in the joint after the pieces to be joined have been pressed together [19].

Related to the size of the contact area is the basic matter of how well contact has been made. It is imperative that all pieces of clay to be joined are pressed together firmly.

19

20

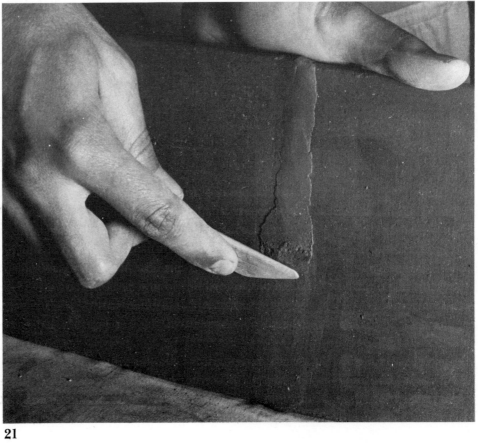

21

A technique that increases the pressure exerted on a joint and that is therefore advisable to use with all types of joints and in all instances is paddling. Paddling—that is, hitting the seam or reinforcing coil gently with a wooden tool—drives the joint together or pushes the reinforcing clay into the seam [20]. In addition, it realigns the clay particles in one direction, which strengthens the joint enormously. I have found that a paddled joint rarely cracks.

I should also stress that it is quite sufficient to reinforce the joint on one side only, either the inside or the outside. The seam can be left showing for a decorative effect (see p. 71), or it may be totally obscured by filling all the indentations with clay and paddling and scraping the surface smooth [21]. Some ceramicists even use a Surform tool to remove all traces of the joint (see pp. 102, 186–87; photo 222).

Firm contact, a large contact area, reinforcement, proper scoring and slipping, as well as paddling, should keep most seams together. But all this has to occur with the proper timing; that

is, when the clay is at the right consistency. While plastic to plastic, plastic to leather-hard, and leather-hard to leather-hard clays can be joined, plastic or leather-hard clay can *never* be joined to bone-dry clay. If the clay cannot be indented with normal pressure from the fingers, it is too hard for other clay to be joined to it permanently.

In general, the harder the clay is, the more endangered the seam. The greater the discrepancy between the water content of the two clay pieces, the greater the chance for cracks to develop, because of the differing degrees of shrinkage of the two pieces.

Even when you observe all the proper procedures and timing considerations, your piece may still crack at the seam. This may be due to fast drying, uneven wall thickness, stressful shapes, etc.

The seam of a piece will always be its weak spot and the first to give, so the attention given to proper joining methods can rarely be overdone.

Wall Thickness

It is difficult to make a general rule about how thick the wall of a ceramic piece ought to be. Wall thickness depends on the clay body, the "look" of the form, and the size of the piece.

For pieces with thick walls, clays that contain grog should be used. A clay body that contains grog is called an *open* body. Grog is fired clay that has been ground into fine particles. Within the clay wall, tiny cracks form around each piece of grog as the clay dries, since the grog does not shrink but the clay around it does. Through these cracks, the moisture can escape from the inside of the wall.

That the thickness of the walls influences the look of a piece is self-evident. A delicate look can rarely be achieved with a thick wall.

With regard to the size of the piece, the larger the piece, the thicker the walls need to be, although the increase in wall thickness is not in direct relation to the increase of the size of the piece. In general, on an average-sized piece (12″–18″ tall), the wall can range from ⅜″ to ½″ in thickness, while the walls of an 8-foot-tall piece may be anywhere from ⅝″ to 1″ thick. On the other hand, I have seen pieces made of clay slabs no thicker than a piece of leather and I

have worked with clay walls as substantial as two inches.

No matter how thick a wall is, however, wall thickness should remain the same throughout the piece. This is an ideal that can and should be adhered to in most cases. When you deal with complex sculptural forms, however, the thickness may have to vary a great deal. When one changes the thickness, one has to take into account not only the structural consequences, because of the change in weight, but also the fact that thicker walls dry more slowly and the rate of shrinkage may therefore vary.

As regards structural stresses, I sometimes deliberately make the walls thinner if a form projects into space, to reduce the stress by making the projection as light as possible. If I need to thicken an area toward the top of a piece, I may reinforce the area below it with clay strips that run vertically all the way down from the top to the floor on the inside.

Careful and slow drying procedures minimize the problem of uneven drying, and a gradual transition from thin to thick helps to alleviate the stress of an uneven rate of shrinkage.

Eventually, all potters develop their own feel for the right wall thickness, and also good judgment as to when and to what extent to break the rule of "even" walls.

Working in Stages

Small pots or forms can often be made in one sitting, but a great number of forms have to be worked in stages to prevent the form from collapsing or sagging under its own weight. In other words, one can only build up to a certain point before one must allow the clay to dry to the leather-hard stage, on the maxim that clay hardens as it dries.

Rules on how far to proceed without stopping cannot be established. A great deal depends on the kind of form being made. Since clay has a great deal of compressive strength—it can support its own weight quite well vertically—a cylindrical form of 8″–10″ in diameter can be built 12″–18″ high without danger of collapsing. If a higher piece is desired, one has to let the bottom dry a bit before proceeding. Cylindrical forms of a diameter wider than 10″ cannot be built as high in each stage.

Forms with abruptly changing diameters, such as spherical forms and forms that go off the vertical [22; white bands indicate stages], often have to be built in numerous stages and allowed to harden every few inches at critical points.

The length of time one has to allow before proceeding depends on the drying conditions, the kind of clay one is working with, and the thickness of the wall (see p. 42 on drying).

23

In order to keep the clay at the very top of the piece moist, and to insure a gradual transition from the leather-hard clay to the plastic clay, I cover the rim with plastic when I stop [23]. This way, I can be sure that no cracks develop between the two stages. In addition, I score and slip before continuing.

On very large pieces, I make sure the form and surface of each section are totally finished before proceeding. Very often, significant changes become difficult to make later, since the clay may become too hard, the weight on top may not allow the clay to be moved, or in some cases the bottom parts may simply not be accessible any more. I paddle each section before proceeding (see pp. 109, 110, 211).

In order to avoid uneven shrinkage, care should be taken that the bottom does not become bone-dry while one is still working on the top. Keep the bottom covered with plastic at all times, once it is leather-hard.

One of the hardest things to learn is to stop building even before a piece threatens to collapse. Unfortunately, the right feel often comes only after many failures.

24

Supports

To woodworkers, metalsmiths, and stone carvers, clay may seem as limp a material as fiber, but clay is stronger than most people realize. As we have discussed, cylinders can be built 18″ high in one step without danger of collapsing. And as clay dries, it becomes stronger and stronger, until, when it is fired, its structural strength is enormous.

We potters do have to admit that there are times when clay needs help. Certain forms at the plastic stage will not stand up without supports, and some forms may even need supports throughout the whole process of building, drying, and firing.

When using temporary or permanent supports, however, a potter must take the shrinkage of the clay into account. For this reason, clay is often the best material one can use for supports, even if it has to be used in big, solid chunks. Clay supports shrink at the same rate as the piece and therefore move with it. If the supports are on the outside of the piece and have to remain there throughout the drying and firing process, I place both the piece and the supports on a clay slab. As the piece shrinks in, the supports are also moved in by the shrinking slab [24].

Certain forms, particularly large ones, need an interior structure that keeps the walls from buckling. This structure has to be built into the piece from the beginning. The interior webbing should be curved, since a curve can respond to stresses by bending. I would also advise that the webbing not just butt against the side but be worked directly into the outer wall [25].

In some cases, supports can be made with materials other than clay. To support a piece while it is progressing from the plastic to the leather-hard stage, almost anything can be used so long as it does not impede the shrinkage of the clay. Blocks of foam rubber are ideal for this purpose (see pp. 170–71; photo 190).

Supports that help in the actual construction of a form are discussed on pages 86–93.

Remember also that clay hardens as it dries and that working in stages may be preferable to using supports.

25

Stickiness of Clay

Wet clay has a tendency to stick to everything. The wetter the clay, the more adhesive it is. As it dries, it loses its stickiness. At the plastic stage, clay should not adhere to your hands any more; it will, however, stick to itself, a fact that we exploit in joining. Plastic clay will also stick to non-absorbent materials or materials of little absorbency, such as wood. The more absorbent a material is, the less likely that clay will adhere to it. At the leather-hard stage, clay will not stick to itself (that is why, in joining, we have to score and slip it) or to non-absorbent material.

In cases where the stickiness of clay is a disadvantage, certain precautions have to be taken. A piece of cloth should always be placed between the clay and your working surface. I always put a cloth underneath each piece of work and beat out all slabs on canvas-covered boards. Some ceramicists use a cloth between the clay and their paddle (see p. 172; photo 194), or even when manipulating the clay (see pp. 171, 172). If I use clay supports, I tend to put small pieces of cloth between the support and the piece, since plastic clay will sometimes stick to leather-hard.

The stickiness of clay is also the reason why most tools are made out of wood. Wood, however, becomes wet quite fast, and then clay will stick to it.

Drying, Wrapping, and Resoftening

Drying is rarely discussed in detail, yet many a piece has been ruined by improper drying methods.

Pots dry from the top down. Except when one is working in stages, the bottom is usually the last part that dries.

The rate at which clay dries depends on several things: (1) the humidity of the air, (2) the openness of the clay, and (3) the type and size of the form.

As for humidity, in the winter on cold dry days, particularly if you have a hot-air heating system, ceramic pieces can dry out completely in a matter of hours, while on hot humid summer days it may take several hours for a pot to reach the leather-hard stage. Clay dries a great deal faster in Albuquerque, New Mexico, than in Trenton, New Jersey.

As regards clay body, size, and type of form, an open clay body (one with grog) dries more rapidly than a dense one, thin walls faster than thick ones, and projections faster than the rest of the piece.

A ceramic piece should always be allowed to dry as evenly as possible; it is a good idea, therefore, to drape plastic over those areas that tend to dry faster.

How fast should a piece be allowed to dry? That depends on a number of things. A pot of average size with even walls can be allowed to dry by simply leaving it uncovered. Composite pieces, pieces with projections, pieces with uneven walls, and pieces with interior clay bracings, etc., should be allowed to dry very, very slowly and from the inside out. This is achieved by covering the piece tightly with thin plastic until all the clay seems to be at the same stage of dryness. It is important to take the plastic off occasionally to shake off the condensation on it. Once the clay is leather-hard, it may be enough to drape the plastic loosely over the piece. When the clay takes on a grayish cast and feels as hard as a board, the plastic can be taken off entirely. For very complex pieces, this process can take from two to four weeks, or longer.

Force drying—that is, putting a piece in the sun, underneath heat lamps, on stoves, etc.—should be done with great care and only if absolutely necessary. This system tends to dry pieces very unevenly and mostly on the surface.

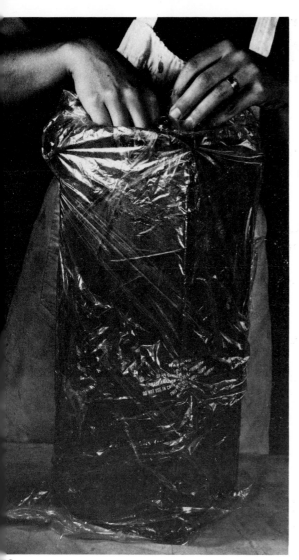

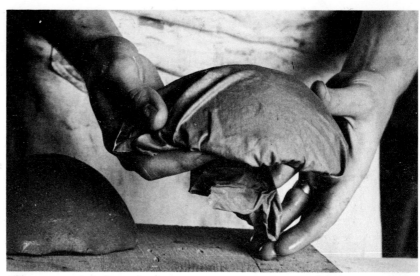

27

6

28

Unnecessary stresses, cracking, and warpage are too often the result.

Pots can be kept damp and in a workable stage for weeks if they are wrapped properly. I use two layers of plastic, one very thin, the other heavier. I spray the thin plastic with a mist of water so that it clings very tightly to the clay all over, like a skin [26]. Then I wrap it in the heavier plastic, secured with clothespins, taking care not to leave any openings where the moisture might escape.

Clay that has become slightly too hard can be resoftened by draping it with a damp (not drip-

ping wet) cloth or paper towel [27] and then with plastic [28]. I let it sit for ten to twenty minutes and then check. If allowed to sit too long, the paper towel or cloth will reabsorb the moisture out of the clay. I would advise this process only for small pieces or the rim or top section of a piece. Never attempt to soften an area that has to support considerable weight. Also be careful that no water runs down the side of your piece and collects at the bottom.

Clay that is too dry to be dented with the pressure of the fingers is usually too hard to soften again.

Responsiveness of Clay

The curse and beauty of clay is its responsiveness. Every time one touches it, one leaves a mark. To the professionals who have learned to discipline themselves, it is a gift, while to the beginner it is a frustrating experience. It is very difficult to learn to touch clay only when absolutely necessary, and to be at all times aware of how to touch it. Ceramicists have a special way of touching clay. It is a searching, feeling, and seeing touch, a touch that is firm, yet gentle. Usually the fingers are slightly arched or straight, with tension throughout. It is not the very tips of the fingers that touch the clay, but the pad, the most sensitive part of the finger.

One cannot be taught that special touch, one has to strive for it until it comes. The look of the clay, the freshness and tension of its surface will tell you whether you have it or not.

Because of the responsiveness of clay, it is essential that both hands work together, one bracing the other or counteracting the pressure of the other.

The responsiveness of the clay also demands that the maker be responsive to the needs of the clay. Successful pieces are the result of a dialogue between the clay and the maker.

Joining, wall thickness, working in stages, supports, the stickiness and responsiveness of clay, drying—these all relate to almost anything you do with clay. The procedures outlined are rooted in the maxims of clay, discussed earlier; namely, that clay is plastic and that it shrinks and hardens as it dries.

The procedures, however, sometimes allow for a great deal of variation and latitude. This is partially due to the fact that there are different kinds of clay bodies with widely varying characteristics, such as shrinkage, plasticity, etc., and also that many terms are relative. Leather-hard, for instance, can only be described in terms of its boundaries—it is a stage between plastic and bone-dry. There are many stages of leather-hard.

The rules and procedures should be used only as guidelines. It is important to know the rules, but they should simply increase one's awareness of the boundaries, and not become restrictive. One might take the attitude that knowing the rules allows one to break them intelligently.

5

Forming Methods

When one thinks of ceramic forms, as I have mentioned before, one has to think almost always in terms of hollow forms. Hollow forms can be achieved in numerous ways.

In discussing the methods and techniques of forming, I will not speak (as is usually done) in terms of coil, slab, pinch, or the use of molds as separate headings, but I will instead group the techniques according to the construction principles of: (1) working from the solid, (2) combining small building units to construct a form, and (3) constructing a piece from one or more large units.

(1) A hollow form can be achieved by starting with a *solid*. The solid can be pierced in some way (thumb or dowel), and the shape is arrived at as the walls are thinned by pressure from the inside and outside. The outside of a form can also be determined as a solid and then cut open at the leather-hard stage and carved out, or a dowel pushed through the thickest part of the piece. In addition, hollow tubular forms can be made from solid clay with the aid of an extruder.

(2) A form can be built by joining *small building units* together. The small units can take numerous forms, such as coils, small slabs, balls of clay, pinches of clay, etc. Proper joining methods are essential in order to avoid cracking later on.

(3) A form can be arrived at by the use of *large building units*. These almost always take the form of slabs that make up the sides of a form or enclose space to make up the entire form. The clay slabs may be plastic or leather-hard. At the plastic stage, the slab may be worked with directly or in conjunction with aids such as supports or molds.

In addition, I will discuss the technique of paddling. *Paddling* is a forming method insofar as it refines and alters a previously made form; it can be used in conjunction with all the other techniques.

None of the work shown in this section should be looked at as a finished product. The emphasis will be on the process rather than the product, in the hope that the process may lead to different products for each reader. It is also hoped that the processes are discussed in terms general enough to lead you into ways of working with clay that are personal and unique.

Forming from the Solid

The methods of forming from the solid fall generally into two categories: (1) where the piece is formed as the clay is thinned, and (2) where the form is finished as a solid and the interior hollow established later. With all the techniques that start from a solid, it is essential that the clay be extremely well wedged, so that there are no air bubbles or uneven parts of clay in terms of its consistency.

Three methods fall into the first category: (1) the pinch method; (2) the dowel method; and (3) the method of extruding shapes with the help of a machine.

Pinch Method

One of the simplest ways to make a hollow shape is to take a ball of clay about the size of a fist, insert one's thumb in the center [29], and thin the wall by squeezing it up and out between the thumb on the inside and the fingers on the outside while turning the pot in one's hand [30, 31].

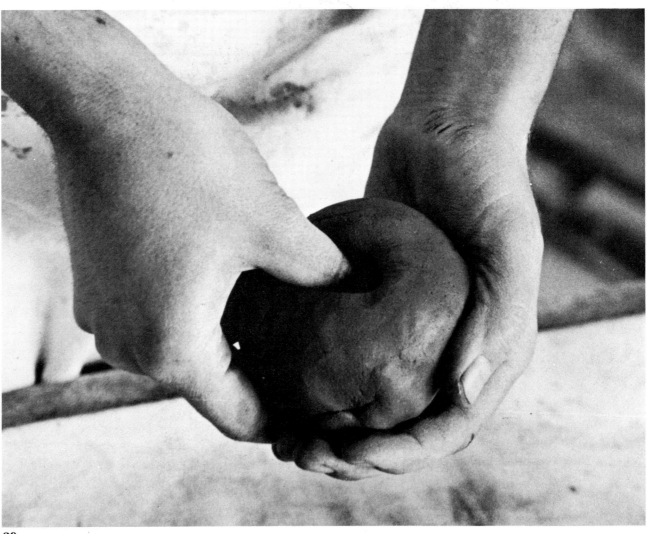

29

30

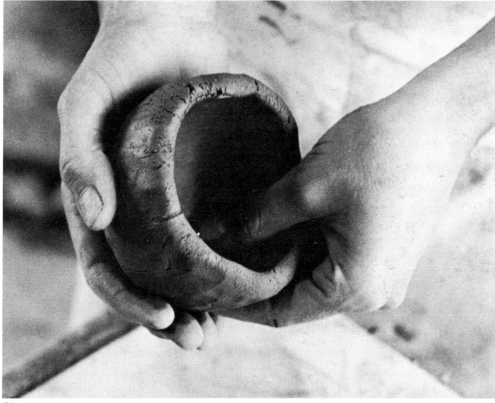

31

32

33

Press the thumb down as far as you can [32], but leave enough clay for the bottom of the form. Then move from the bottom to the rim in small steps, each time squeezing the clay gently between the thumb on the inside and the fingers on the outside [33]. It is important to squeeze gently, so that the wall is thinned a little at a time. After reaching the rim, turn the pot about one-quarter of an inch and thin the wall again from the bottom up. Repeat this procedure until the entire pot is as thin as you desire. This thinning procedure should take several revolutions, since you only thin the wall a little at a time.

The wall can be thinned further by pulling the clay up with the thumb, moving in one motion from the bottom to the rim [34]. The shape can be bulged out in places, using the same pulling action [35].

Although this technique is simple, one has to develop a sensitivity to the clay and an ability to judge the thickness of the wall with one's fingers. Observe carefully the response of the clay to the pressure of your fingers and the manner in which the clay moves. It is a good idea to work with your eyes closed, in order to develop a feel for the clay.

The forms that can be made by this technique are obviously limited in size but not in expression. Paulus Berensohn, in *Finding One's Way with Clay,* which is devoted entirely to this technique, discusses thoroughly the whole range of possibilities. For instance, by deliberately starting off-center, one can change the visual balance; the rim can be treated in many different ways, and the surface can be paddled, scraped, or textured. The forms can be opened wide or closed. In addition, several forms can be combined to form a more complex one.

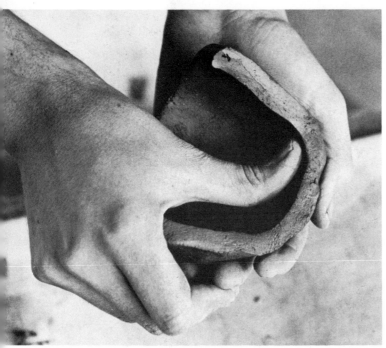

34

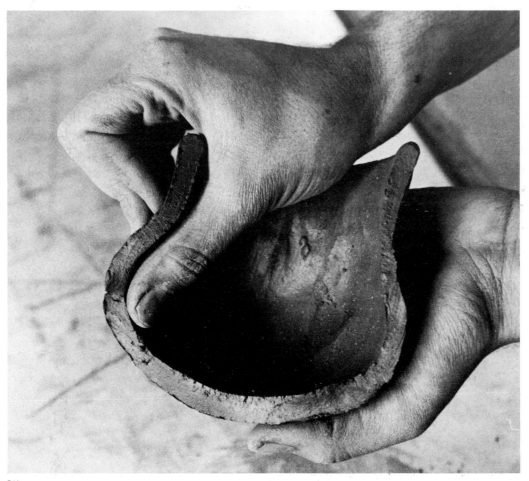

35

36

Dowel Method

Another way to make a form from a solid is to insert a dowel through the center of a cylindrical or conical block of clay [36] and thin the walls by rolling the clay on the table [37, 38]. The pressure against the clay from the dowel on the inside and from the table on the outside squeezes the clay and stretches it horizontally. In other words, the diameter of the cylinder is widened; it does not gain in height.

Great care has to be taken that the wall is thinned evenly, and it helps to replace the dowel with a thicker one as the opening becomes larger [38].

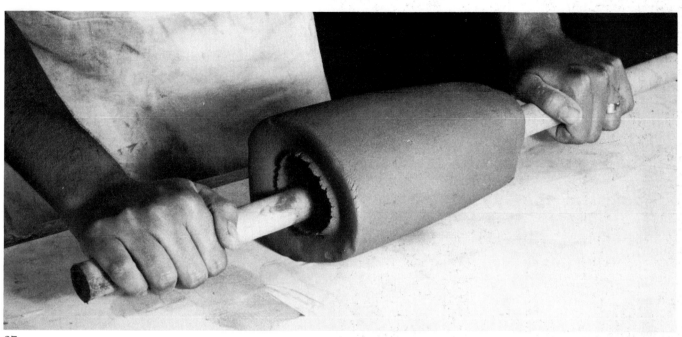

37

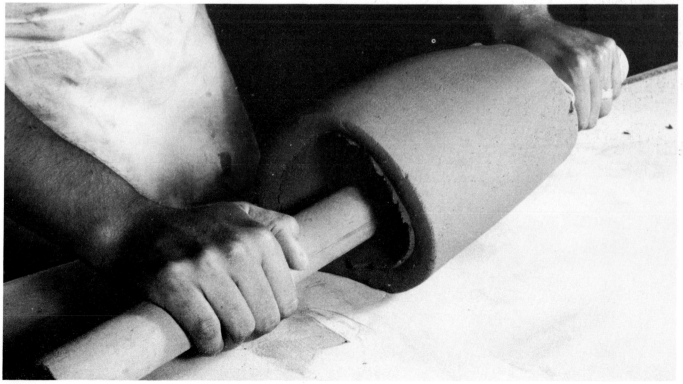

38

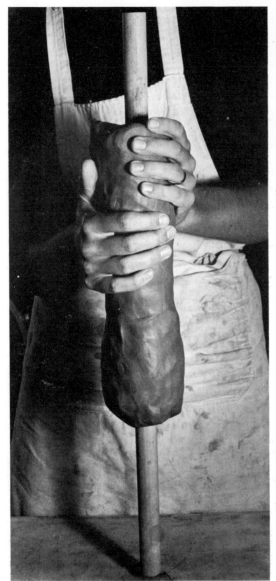

39   40

At first, it may be difficult to judge the relationship of the width to the height of the pot. The thicker the solid cylinder of clay, the more the clay can be thinned, and the wider the hollow cylinder will be. With tall cylinders, it is difficult to push the dowel through the exact center. In this case, start with a fatter but shorter cylinder of clay, push the dowel through, and then thin the cylinder and elongate it, by

pushing the clay up on the dowel with both hands [39].

This technique, like the pinch method, clearly exploits the plasticity of the clay. The clay is stretched, and the resulting texture can be very exciting. The forms are simple, cylindrical or conical, yet can be very subtle in the way the curve changes. The rim also reflects the forces exerted on the clay; and no amount of modeling could achieve its subtlety [40].

Bottoms can be added in the form of a slab, or one end may be squeezed together.

Extruded Forms

Making forms with an extruder is becoming increasingly popular. An extruder is an industrial device that can be adapted to creative uses in many different ways. The extruder consists of a tube through which clay is pushed by a plunger that is attached to a jack or lever. The clay passes a die that forces it into tubular forms. These forms may be of different diameters and may be hollow or solid, depending on the die. Square or other shapes are also possible.

The length of the extruded form is unlimited, but there are certain restrictions on the width, at least in extruders built for studio purposes.

Ceramicists mostly use the extruder to make a basic form quickly that they can then work

with both for functional and for sculptural purposes (see p. 195; photo 232).

Hollowing-out Method

Sculptors for a long time have used the method of making forms as solids, then hollowing them out once they are finished. Potters, on the other hand, have scorned this approach, because the carving-out process seems to negate the plastic quality of the clay and to waste material. The "wasted" clay, however, can be reprocessed and the plastic quality of clay can be fully exploited when one shapes a solid piece of clay. A solid block of clay reacts to pressures differently than a hollow form. Many different kinds of forms, curved planes, and textures are possible.

If the piece is quite thick, it is necessary to cut it open, hollow it out, and rejoin the pieces [41]. This cut has to be worked into the design of the form. At times, when working with

41

42

shallow forms, for instance, it may be sufficient to push a dowel through the thickest part of the piece [42].

Relatively few handbuilding techniques start with the solid. The most commonly used technique in ceramics that does is wheelthrowing. I deal with wheel throwing exclusively in my previous book, *Pottery on the Wheel*.

Forming with Small Building Units

Whereas forms built from the solid have few seams or none at all, the use of small building units results in a network of seams.

I will first discuss how to make some of the building units and then suggest ways to put them together.

In addition, I will discuss a technique developed by Dr. Robert Ramsey of California State University at Long Beach. I call it the "extended pinch method." It combines the method of thinning clay on the form, as is done when working with a solid, with the principles of using small units.

Ceramic forms can be built, very much like a brick house, by joining small units together. These units can be in the form of coils, slabs, pinches, or balls.

Making Small Building Units: Coils and Slabs

Coils are made by rolling clay on the table. Start out by squeezing clay in your hand to form a rough fat coil [43]. Then roll this coil back and forth on the table, giving it its momentum with

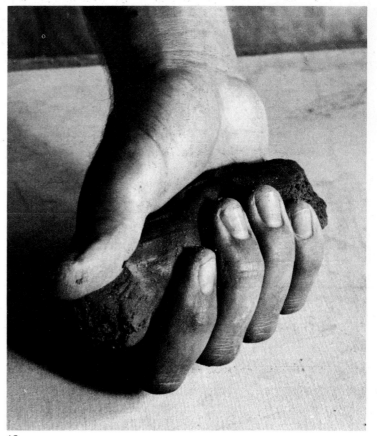

43

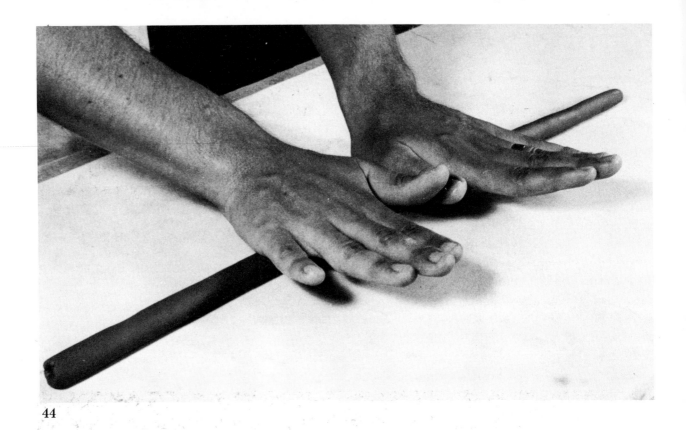

44

the full length of the inside of the hands [44]. To keep the coil from flattening out, it is important that you do not press down too hard and that the coil make at least one complete rotation as it is pushed in one direction.

To make a long coil use more clay, and when rolling, start with your hands in the center and move them apart to either end of the coil. The table surface should be absorbent, and it is a good idea to start with rather moist clay. Rolling dries out the surface of the clay, which causes the coil to crack when one is bending it. Roll only as long as it is absolutely necessary.

If one uses stiff clay, cavities may form inside the coil [45]. Do not use these coils. The air bubbles will burst in the kiln.

45

Slabs. Small slabs can be made in a number of ways. I will describe the most common ones, which are: (1) beating out a slab, (2) throwing it out, and (3) using two sticks and a rolling pin.

When beating out a slab, I first flatten a ball of clay by putting my weight on the palm and heel of my hand and pressing down [46] (remember to have a cloth underneath). Then, starting in the center and going to the edges in

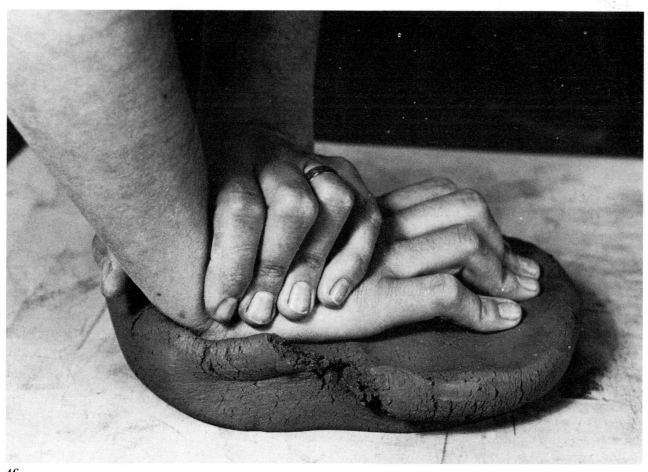

46

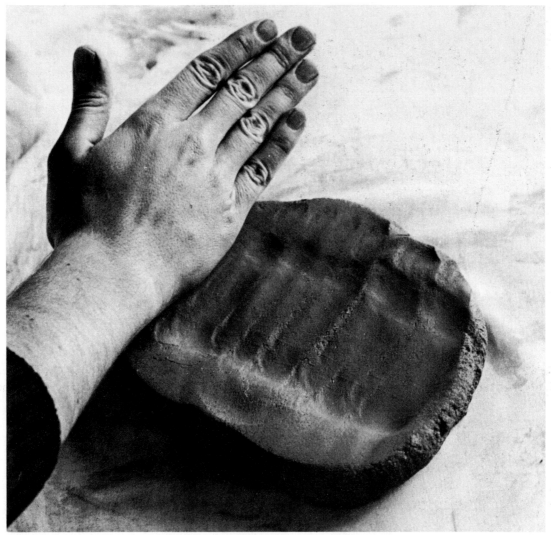

47

all directions, I thin the slab by hitting the clay in short strokes with the side edge of my palm, coming down at an acute angle in closely spaced intervals [47, 48]. I avoid deep indentations, and move the clay from the center out a little at a time. If I want to come from the center toward me, I use the heel of my palm [49]. I stop short of the edge, to prevent it from becoming too thin. I frequently turn the slab over and repeat the beating until the slab is as thin as I want. With some practice, it is possible to get very even slabs in this manner. If I require a perfectly smooth slab, I may go over it with a rolling pin, rolling in all directions to avoid setting up stresses [50].

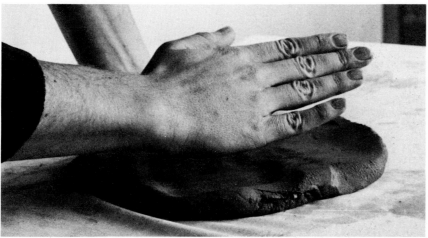

48

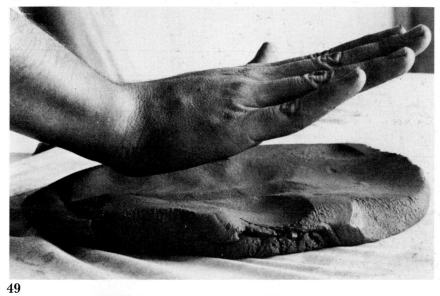

49

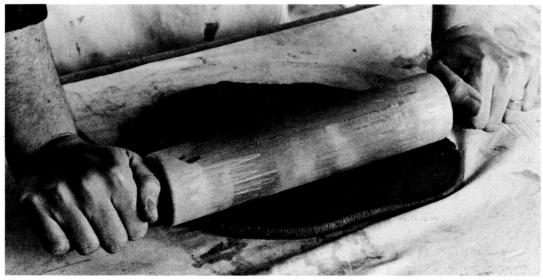

50

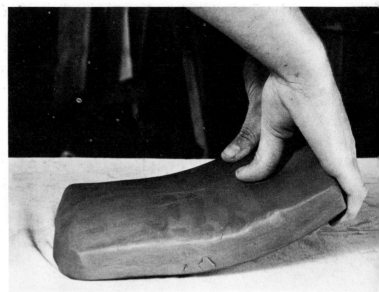

52

51

Some ceramicists prefer to make a slab by throwing. Make a block-like form with the clay [51]. Lay it on the table and grasp the edge farthest away from you [52], lift the clay and, pulling toward you, throw the clay down [53]. In this throwing action, the top side of the slab becomes the bottom side, and the part closest to you becomes the part farthest away from you. The part closest to you when you pick up the slab must touch the table first when you throw it down. Repeat the throwing as often as necessary, but in between throws straighten out the edges by pounding them gently on the table. This way, the edges do not thin more than the rest of the slab [54]. The surface that you throw the slab on should be highly absorbent; otherwise, the clay will stick to it.

This procedure of throwing slabs can produce very thin and even slabs rapidly. The slabs also tend to have an interesting surface that results from the stretching of the clay. In order for the clay to stretch evenly, it is crucial that the clay be extremely well wedged.

53

54

55

A slab can also be made with a rolling pin and two sticks the thickness of the slab. Place a partially flattened mass of clay in between the sticks (with a cloth underneath the clay), and roll until the edges of the rolling pin touch the sticks [55]. The problem with this technique of making slabs is that one stretches the clay in one direction only, and this may set up stresses that may make the slab warp in the drying and firing.

Building with Small Building Units

Let us now turn to combining these units. To make the pot, one usually starts with a slab as the bottom. The first row of building units is added on top of it and joined to the bottom with a reinforcing coil (butt joint) [56]. The building

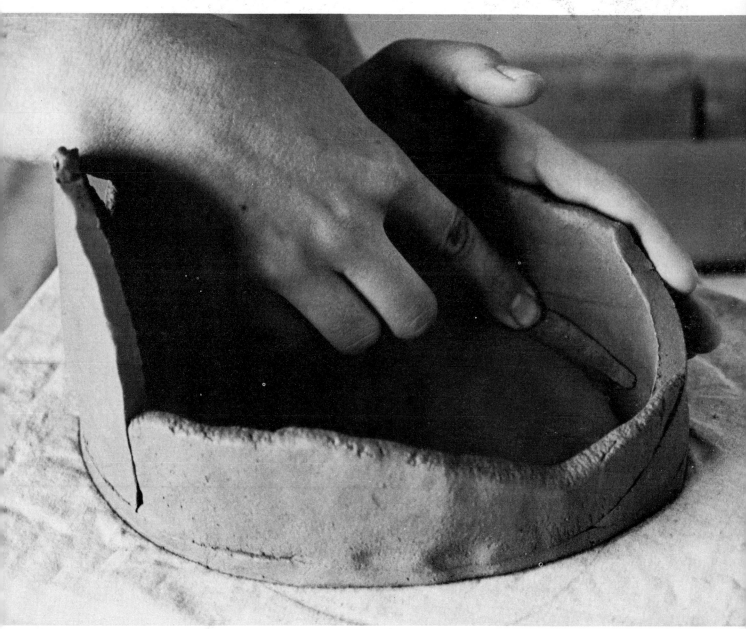

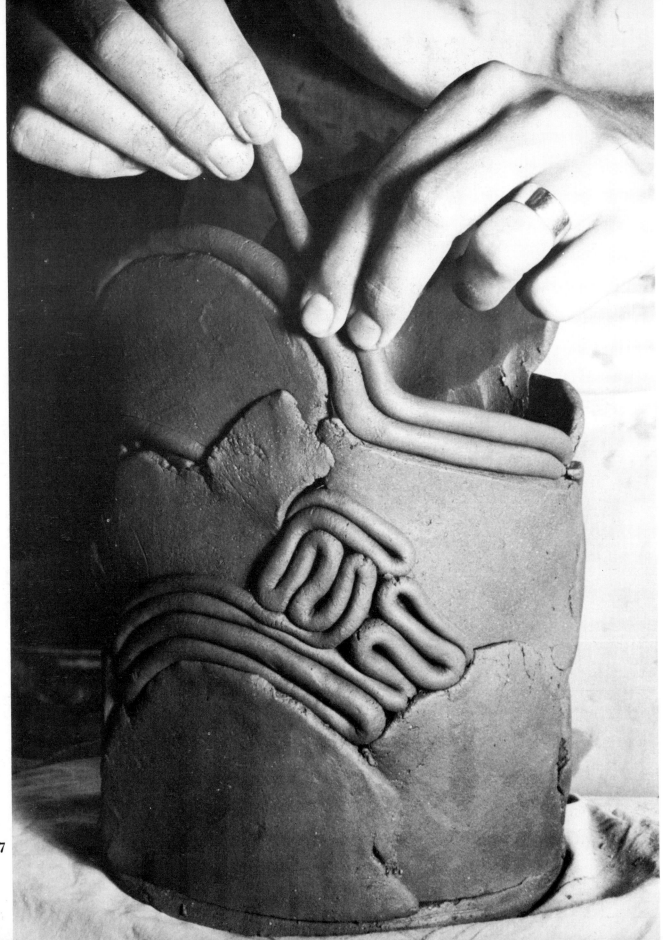

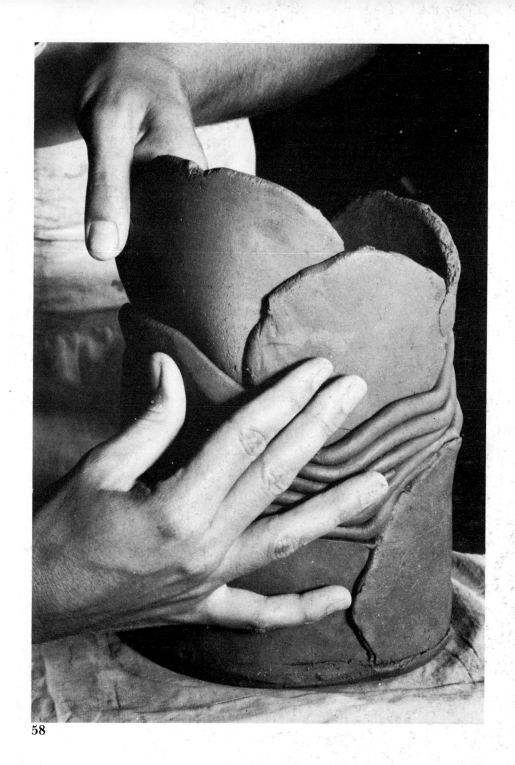

58

units may butt on top or next to each other [57] or overlap [58]. When placing the units, make sure they are pushed firmly together, so that the contact is well established. Use the flexibility of the clay to adjust the units to each other.

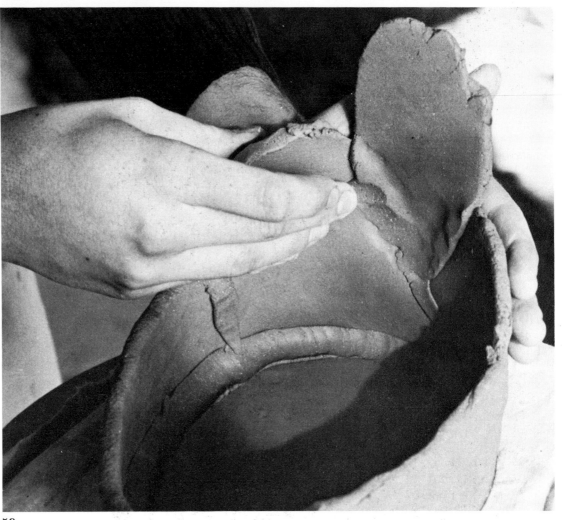

59

The joining method is dictated by the kind of joint: reinforcement in the case of butt joints, or pressing the overlap joint together and moving clay from one side to the other [59].

Coils butt on top of each other, and if they are too thin for clay to be smeared from one to the other, several rows of coils can be joined at the same time by smearing a layer of clay at least an eighth of an inch thick over the entire area. Start with a small ball of clay, flatten it slightly, and smear it from the center of the ball outward onto the coils [60]. Partially overlap each rein-forcement with the previous one [61]. Cover the entire area, not just small parts of it. Do not be tempted, in order to save time, to use flat slabs rather than small balls, as the slabs may trap air.

Note how both hands work together at all times, with one hand counteracting the pressure from one side by supporting the wall on the other [59].

As pointed out, joining need be done on one side only, and if one wishes, one can leave the joints showing on the outside for a decorative effect.

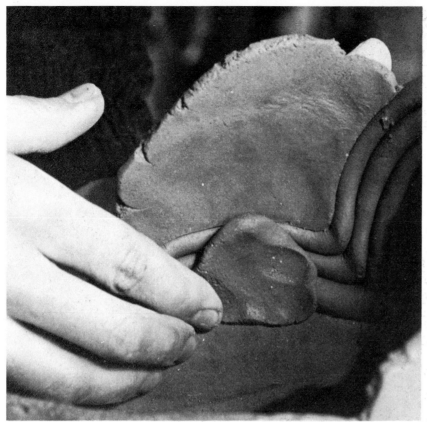

60

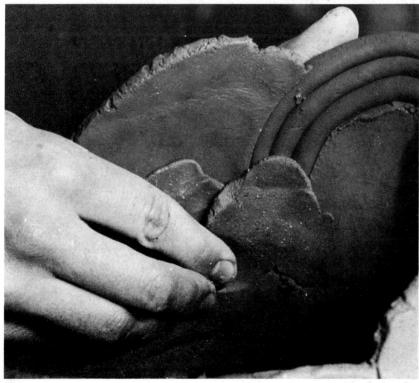

61

62

Coils can also be joined on the outside in a decorative manner with the use of a tool or finger [62].

Openings can be left for functional purposes or for decorative effect. To leave several small openings surrounded by larger solid areas is, of course, structurally sounder than leaving large openings within small solid areas [63].

If you have to work in stages, remember to cover the top edge in plastic and to score and slip before continuing. I also find it helpful to paddle the inside slightly to strengthen the joints, but only once the clay is leather-hard, to avoid distorting the form or changing the shape of the building units. Don't forget to support the wall on the other side with your hand while paddling.

64

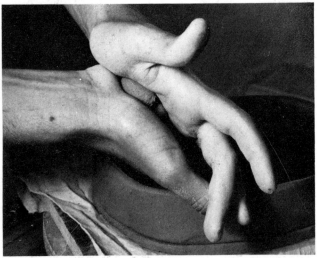

65

Extended Pinch Method

Building with small units and leaving the joints
showing can result in an exciting texture or
pattern. This, however, may not be appropriate
for all forms and purposes. If I desire a smooth
or almost smooth surface, I use the extended
pinch method, which could also be called the
"knitting method," since it consists of interlocking small pieces of clay.

The bottom is made of a slab, and the first
row is a flattened coil secured to the bottom with
a reinforcing coil. Small pieces of clay are
pinched off a chunk of clay [64], flattened
slightly between the palms [65], and added to the
flattened coil, with one-third of the pinch overlapping the coil [66]. The resulting double
thickness is then pushed up, with the thumbs of
both hands on the outside pressing against the
fingers on the inside of the pot [67]. The two
thumbs squeeze toward each other and upward.
The pressure is applied in several closely spaced
steps, starting at the bottom of the pinch and
moving to the top, until the wall thickness feels
even. Note how the rim of the previous row
rises. If you properly squeeze the thumbs toward
each other, you will form a vertical ridge in the
center of the pinch [68]. Even out this ridge and

66

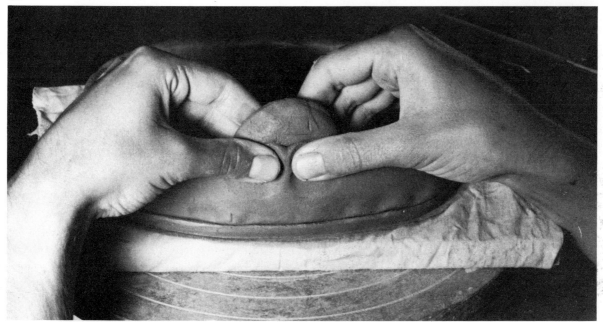

67

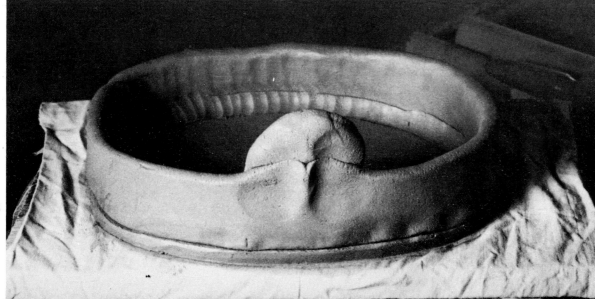

68

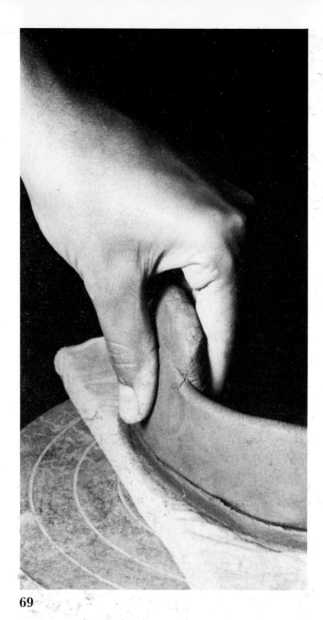

69

any other excessive wall thickness by squeezing the clay gently between the fingers on the inside and the thumbs on the outside. Note that the thumbs and fingers are stretched out and parallel to each other and that their full length is used [**69**].

It is important to push up and not out, and to make sure that no thin spots are created. One has to feel for thick areas and apply just enough pressure to make the wall even. Where it is thin, do not press.

Successive pinches of clay are added, each overlapping both the one beneath it and the one next to it [**70**]. Thin each pinch as it is added. Complete one layer all around, and then start the next row [**71**].

Always work on the part of the pot closest to you. Keep turning the pot, or, on a large piece, walk around it. The initial size and shape of the pinches of clay are relatively unimportant, since they are thinned out and adjusted on the ceramic form. It is, however, easier to work with small pinches than with large ones.

The extended pinch method takes a little bit of practice to learn. It is a good idea first to attempt a straight cylinder, which you cut vertically in half to check for unevenness. If the cylinder widens in diameter toward the top without your having intended it to do so, you are pushing out rather than up.

Once mastered, this technique is extremely fast, since no additional joining is necessary. In fact, the only disadvantage is that it is so fast that one tends to go beyond the point where one ought to stop to let the clay become leather-hard. When I work in stages, I thin the top of the last row to less than half the desired wall thickness, in preparation for the next stage. Ordinarily, one thins the top of the last row and the added pinch simultaneously. When you begin a new stage, however, the last row cannot be thinned easily, since it is somewhat leather-hard. I score and slip before continuing the next stage, even though the top edge was covered with plastic.

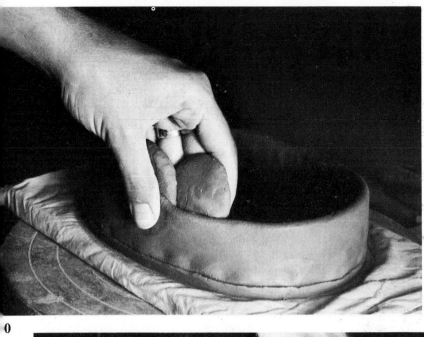

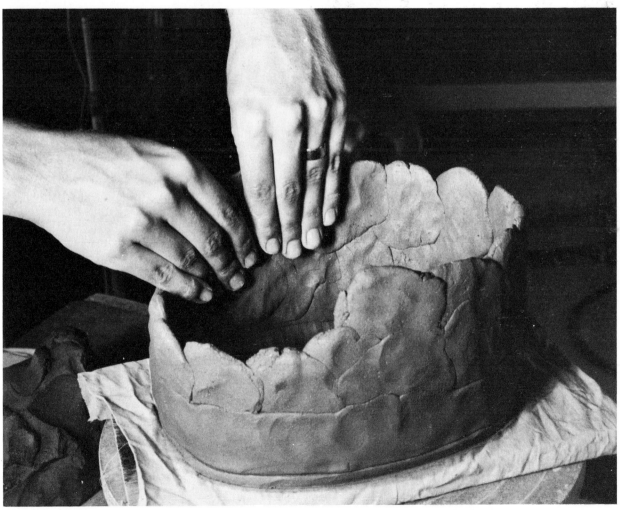

70

71

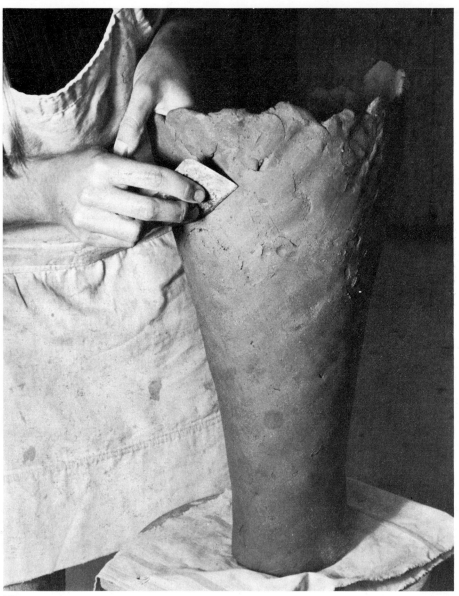

72

Because of the interlocking pinches, the walls are very strong. This technique is suitable for any kind of shape of any size. The texture and form can be refined by paddling at the leather-hard stage (see pp. 109, 110; photos 127, 128), or a smooth surface can be achieved by scraping it with a flexible rib after every few rows [72].

The various techniques of building forms with small units can be easily mastered and offer a great variety of possibilities: the units can be small and delicate, hard-edged and geometric, or torn and free-flowing. Large forms can be built as easily as small ones. Simple cylindrical forms, swelling round forms, as well as complex composite forms, are possible. At the beginning, these techniques may try your patience. However, with increased dexterity, progress becomes more rapid.

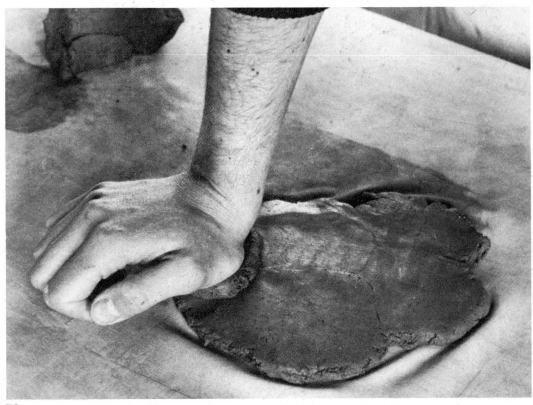

73

Forming with Large Building Units

More rapid, but often more complex than building with small units, is building a piece from one or several large units. The form that this unit takes is quite often a slab, or, as we shall see, a form made from a slab.

I will first discuss how large slabs can be made

and then the various ways in which one can work with them.

Making Large Slabs

Making large slabs can be laborious and tiring. It is somewhat easier if you "build" the slab, by overlapping handfuls of clay [73] and then thinning them one at a time with the side and heel of your hand in the manner I described for small slabs (pp. 59–61). As with small slabs, you can roll a large slab smooth with a rolling pin.

74

Some ceramicists throw out large slabs using
the same method that is described for small
slabs (pp. 62–63). This, however, takes quite a
bit of experience.

In order to make slabs of perfectly even thickness, one can use a slab board. This consists of a
canvas-covered board with two wooden sticks the
thickness of the slab nailed to the edges [74]. I
beat clay into the slab board by overlapping
handfuls of clay and beating them together with
the heel or the side of my hand. I try to get as
close to the desired thickness as possible. The
excess clay is removed in the following manner.
First, any clay on the wooden stick is removed
[75]. Then, riding on the two sticks at the edges,
I rotate a straight-edged board back and forth
three or four inches around a central point [76].
This is repeated every five inches, until ridges
are created over the whole slab [77] that can be

75

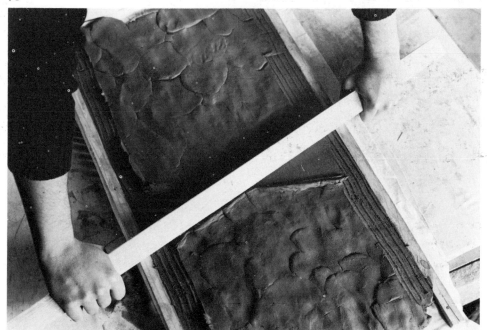

76

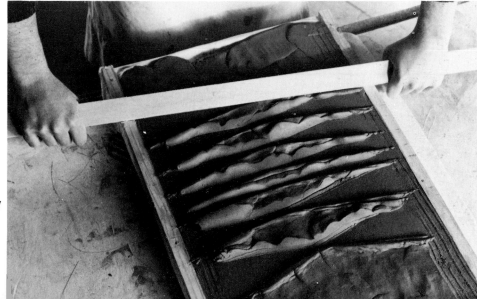

77

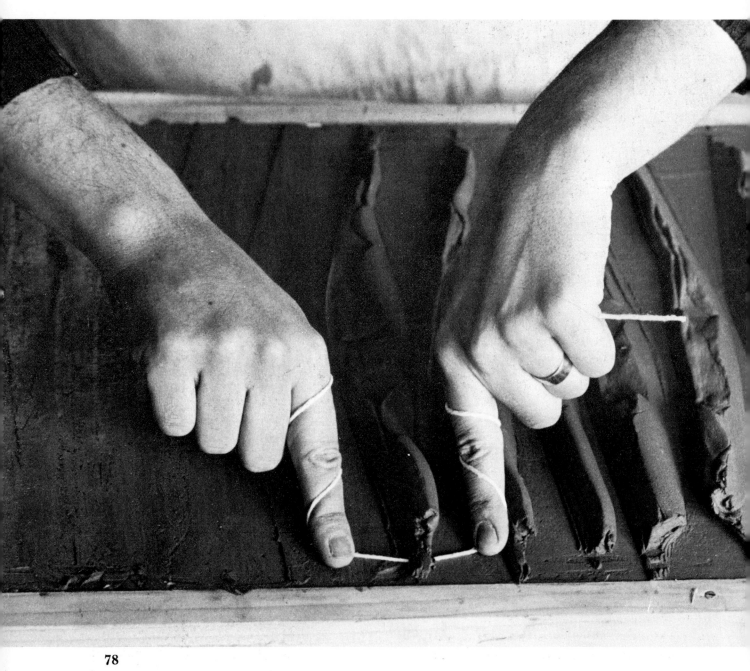

78

79

cut off with a wire or string [78]. Any excess clay is then removed by pulling the straight-edged board across the top of the clay, using the sticks as guides [79]. The texture can be smoothed by rolling the slab with a thick dowel or rolling pin.

Most convenient, and a tremendous work saver, is a slab roller. This is, unfortunately, a relatively expensive machine that forces the clay through rollers, thinning it to whatever thickness you desire. Slab rollers save time and work, and some ceramicists report that they produce slabs that are less likely to warp [80].

Once the slabs are prepared, they can be worked with at two stages—the plastic and the leather-hard.

80

Douglas Hopkins

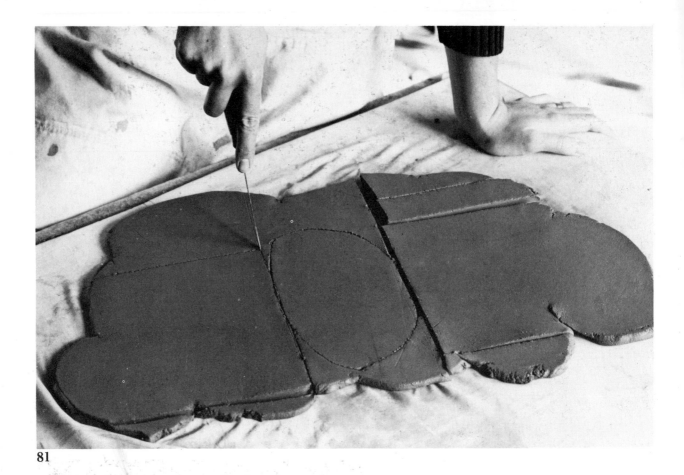

81

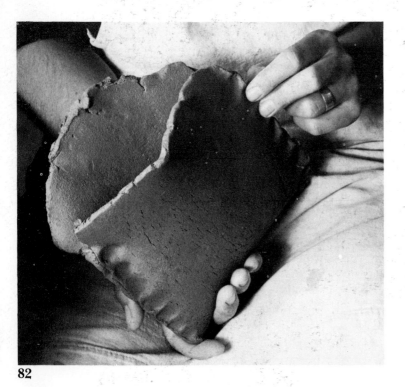

82

Building with Plastic Slabs

A plastic slab has all the good and also all the less desirable qualities of clay. Its plasticity allows it to be bent and formed in many different ways, but its lack of structural strength limits its use. Up to a point, then, plastic clay slabs can be worked directly, but quite frequently ceramicists use some aids that help them in achieving forms with the slab that would be difficult if not impossible, to obtain otherwise.

Directly. Working directly with a plastic slab gives one a great deal of flexibility. Pots can be made very rapidly by using slabs for the sides and bottom [81], or by making the whole pot out of one slab [82]. The sides can be joined either by an overlap joint [83] or by a butt joint [84], leaving the joint showing or obscuring it by smoothing it over [85]. When attaching a bottom

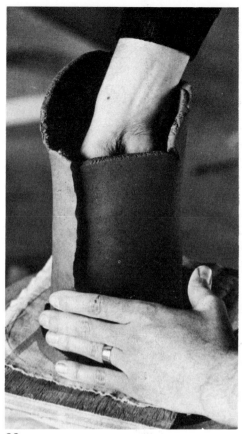

83

84

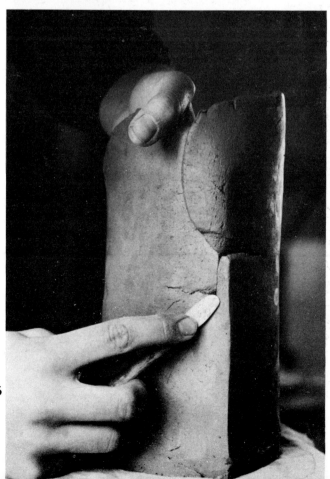

85

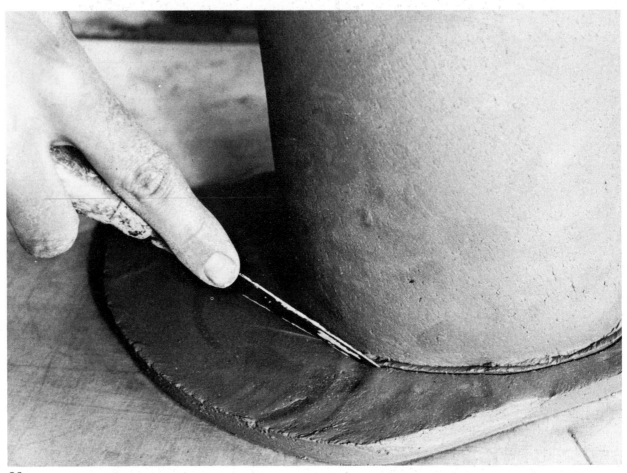

86

that cannot be reached easily on the inside to reinforce it with a coil, it is a good idea to make the bottom one-quarter of an inch larger [86] and to work this excess clay into the sides [87].

When working with slabs at the plastic stage, one has to be aware that the plastic clay responds to every touch. It is therefore necessary to develop that "certain" touch for clay (see p. 44), in order to retain the freshness and avoid a touched-up or overworked look.

Working with plastic slabs can be very exciting. Spontaneity and fluidity characterize the best pieces made in this manner.

87

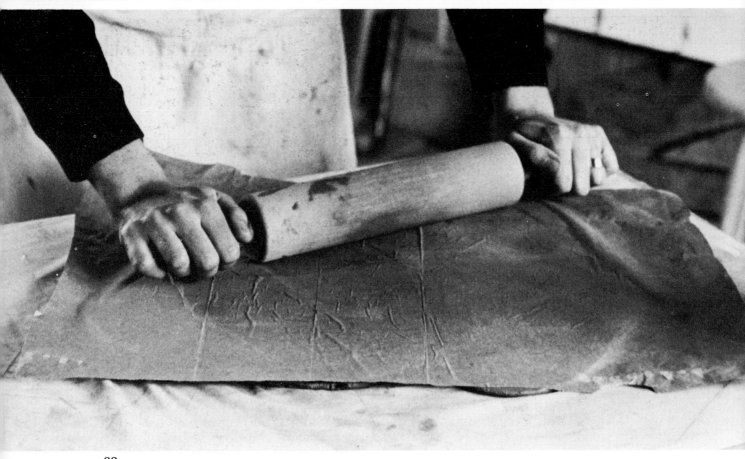

88

With aids. Very large slabs are difficult to handle at the plastic stage because they tend to sag and tear under their own weight. One of several ways to strengthen a clay slab is to mix short strands of thin fibers into the wet clay. This can be done by wedging them in or by adding them to the mixture when the clay is initially mixed.

Attaching brown wrapping or butcher paper or a sheet of plastic to the slab also strengthens it. Dampen the clay slab with a sponge and then firmly roll or rub on the paper or plastic [88]. Use scissors to cut the clay in both cases. Remove the paper or plastic when the pieces are assembled.

While these methods alleviate the problem of the slab tearing while it is handled, they do not increase the structural strength of the clay. For this purpose, ceramicists have devised a number of aids that often fulfill two functions at the same time. Most of these aids help in the construction of a form that is otherwise difficult, if not impossible, to achieve, by supporting the clay until its structural strength has increased in drying, so that it can support itself. Some aids, in addition to being supports, make it possible to duplicate a size and shape over and over again.

Supports. When devising aids that act as supports, several considerations have to be taken into account. (1) The supports can never be allowed to be in the way of the shrinking clay. As discussed earlier, the supports have to be either pliable enough so that the shrinking clay

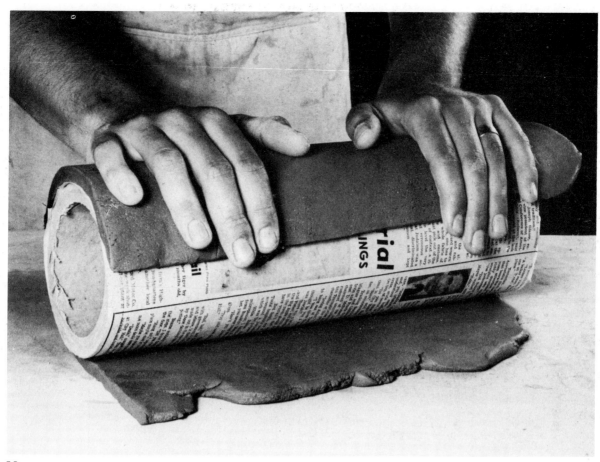

89

can compress them or they have to be used in such a way that they do not impede the shrinkage of the clay. (2) The supports may have to be positioned in such a way that they can be removed once the clay can support itself. In the case of combustible supports, they can be burned out in the firing, but only if a fuel-burning kiln is used. Smoke can severely damage the elements in an electric kiln. (3) Clay will stick to non-absorbent or minimally absorbent materials. If your support is of such a material, a piece of paper or cloth should be put in between the clay and the support as a separator.

Here are some suggestions for supports. A plastic slab of clay can be rolled around a cardboard tube [89]. The cardboard tube should first be lined with paper to prevent the clay from

90

91

92

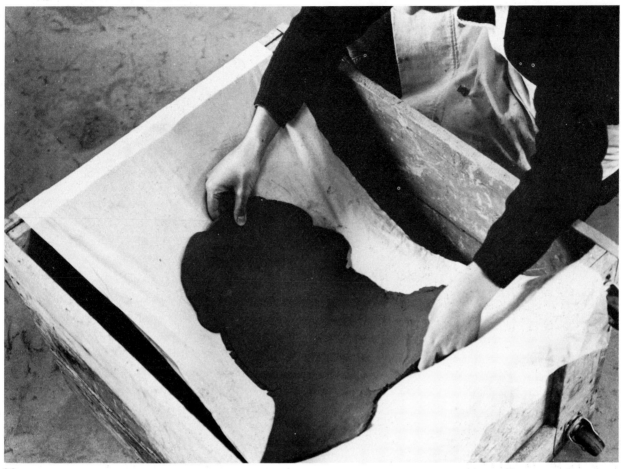

93

sticking to it. The tube has to be removed almost immediately unless it has been surrounded with some foam rubber that will compress enough to let the clay shrink [90]. Because of its springiness, foam rubber can be used as support in a variety of circumstances [91]. Wadded newspaper will act as a support from the inside (yet will compress to allow the clay to shrink) [92]. A hammock made of cloth and suspended inside a box or any other structure will support a curved slab or form until it is leather-hard [93].

The use of a hammock is particularly practical, since it does not impede the shrinkage of the clay. Air on the inside of a totally closed form also acts as a good support. Once the clay begins to shrink, however, you have to provide a hole through which the excess air can escape.

These are just a few examples of the way supports can be used. As long as you keep in mind that clay shrinks as it dries and that it sticks to non-absorbent materials, you can devise your own ways of supporting your forms.

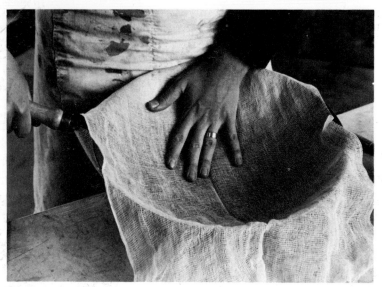

94

Duplication. To duplicate forms over and over again, industry has perfected the technique of molds. The principle, however, was used long before the Industrial Age. Pre-Columbian ceramicists, for instance, used bisqued forms for molds, since bisque ware is very absorbent. The contemporary potter uses a number of different kinds of molds, not just for mass production, but also to make certain forms that are hard to achieve without molds, or that he or she can use over and over again as a basic form that can be altered, embellished, or combined with others.

It is in this context that I will discuss the press mold and the hump or drape mold.

In the case of the *press mold,* the interior of a form is used. The clay is pressed into the forms either by lining the interior with small units of clay [95] or by gently pressing a slab into it [96]. Almost anything can be used for a press mold, but in choosing a mold, there are two important considerations to bear in mind. (1) The opening of the press mold should be equal to the largest diameter of the interior space; otherwise, the press mold has to be broken in order to get the clay form out. (2) The press mold has to be lined with cloth or paper, unless it is so absorbent that the clay will not stick to it (as is the case with a mold made from plaster). Cheesecloth makes a perfect liner for any mold that has little or no absorbency. It stretches in different directions and avoids the imprint that the folds of other cloths leave [94]. (Sometimes, though, such folds can be interesting.)

Once the interior has been lined with an even layer of clay, the clay can be allowed to dry in the mold to either the leather-hard or the bone-dry stage, depending on what one wants to do with it. Certain shapes can even be taken out immediately. Half spheres, for instance, hold their shape if placed on the edge [98] and if they are not handled. To get the form out of the mold, it is best to flip it over with the help of a board [97].

95

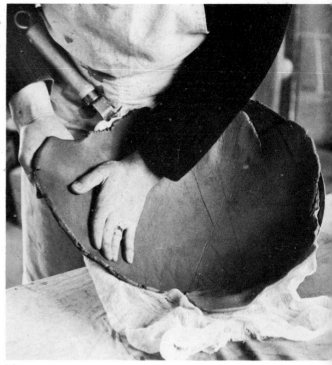

96

97

98

In the case of the *drape* or *hump mold,* the exterior of the mold is used [99]. Again, almost anything can be used for a mold: small forms made of solid clay, household items, or forms made of plaster.

The same considerations have to be kept in mind as with the press mold—namely, the shape of the mold and the material that it is made of. So far as the shape of the mold is concerned, there cannot be any undercuts—it cannot diminish in size from top to bottom—which would prevent lifting the form off the mold. If the mold is rather high, a dart-like cut may have to be made to adjust the slab to the form [100]. However, most of the time the slab can be stretched to adjust to the form [102]. If the material that the mold is made out of has no or little absorbency, a liner has to be used [101].

99

100

101

102

The problem with a drape or hump mold is that it does not allow the clay to shrink (unless a layer of foam rubber is used underneath). The piece, therefore, has to be lifted off as soon as possible. If both hands are used for this [103], and the piece is set down on the cut edge, almost no distortion will occur.

Other items than molds can be used for duplicating forms. Aids, such as the ones discussed under "supports" (pp. 87–89), help in making forms that may not be exactly alike but are similar enough for one's type of work.

Both support aids and molds greatly enlarge the repertoire of ceramic forms, particularly if one views these methods as starting points in the process of making a piece. Many of these shapes can be combined with each other, continued by some other method, or changed and refined by paddling.

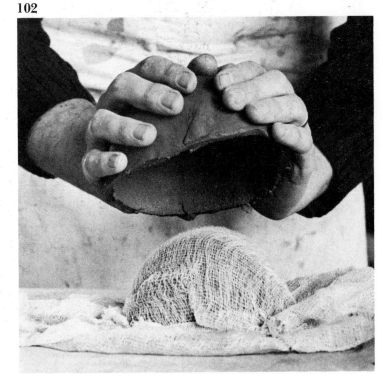

103

104

105

Making Plaster Molds

A great number of objects can be used as molds. If work is done extensively with them, plaster molds are convenient because of their absorbency. They can be made with relative ease, and with careful handling they will last a long time.

First, find a form that can serve as a model, modify a form with the use of clay [104], or make the entire model out of clay. Set the model on a flat, clean surface and place a coil around it about one half inch away from the form. Then

106

107

cover everything, including the table surface and the coil, with Vaseline [105]. To mix the plaster, follow the instructions on the plaster box or use the following procedure. Add the plaster to cold water by sprinkling it evenly over the entire surface. Do this until small islands of plaster appear out of the water [106]. Only then insert your hand into the mixture and gently mix the plaster and water by moving your entire hand under the water [107]. When the mixture has been sufficiently stirred, wait for it to

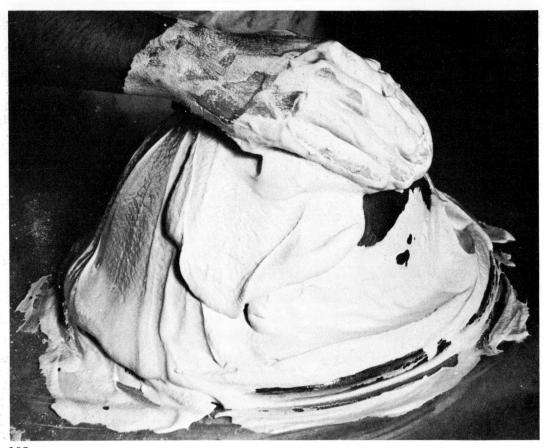

108

thicken slightly and then work it over the form, building up a thickness of at least one half inch [108]. Make sure that the plaster does not run over the outside of the clay coil but ends up on top of it. Scrape the plaster smooth as it sets up [109]. When the plaster has hardened and dried, the form and the clay coil can be taken out and the mold refined by scraping and sanding it. Round off all the edges with a file. The space left by the clay coil provides a convenient undercut for lifting the mold [110]. With the inside and outside sanded smooth, this type of mold can be used either as a drape mold or as a press mold.

To make the plaster slabs for reprocessing clay and wedging, follow the instructions for mixing the plaster. When the plaster starts to thicken just slightly, pour the mixture into a previously prepared form. The form should be sturdy and without leaks. And don't forget to cover the form with Vaseline, or the plaster will stick to it.

Even though plaster, because of its high capacity for absorbing water, is the ideal material for molds and wedging boards, one has to be very avoid any contamination of the clay with plaster. careful, when working with clay on plaster, to Plaster continuously absorbs water and swells in the process. This means that even the tiniest chip of plaster in a clay wall can later cause a rather large chip of clay to pop out.

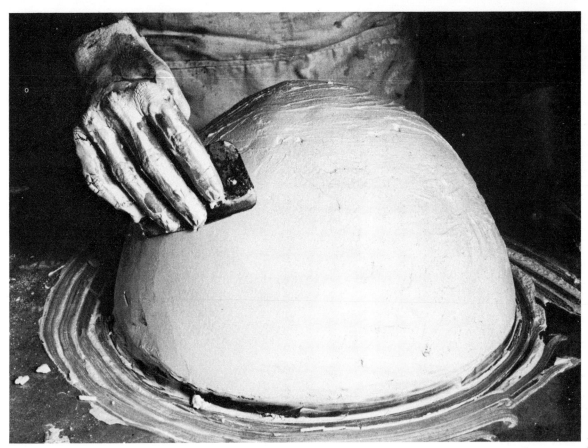

109

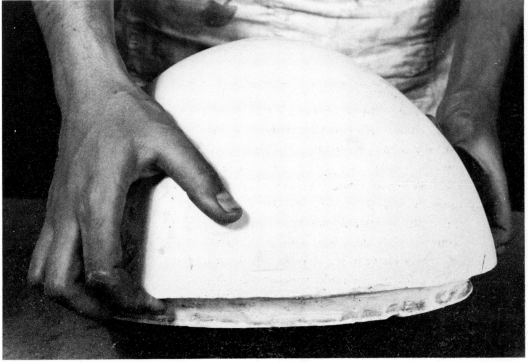

110

111

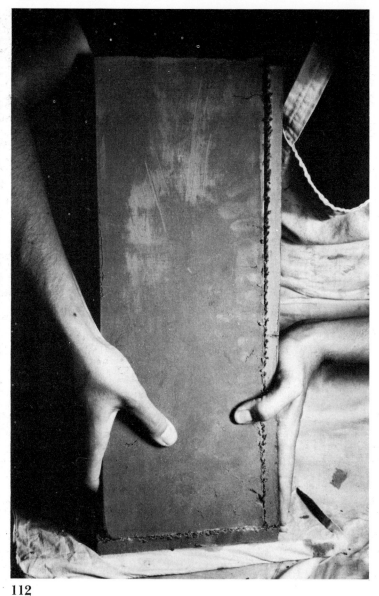

112

Building with Leather-Hard, Large Slabs

Leather-hard is the stage between plastic and bone-dry. At that point, the clay has been allowed to lose some of its plasticity for the sake of structural strength. Leather-hard, however, is a relative term. It can mean anywhere from partial loss of plasticity and some gain in strength to almost total loss of plasticity and a structural strength approaching that of wood.

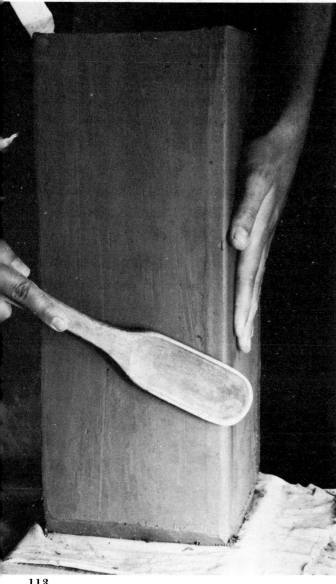

113

114

Leather-hard clay acts and reacts differently than plastic clay and therefore has to be treated and thought of differently. The increased structural strength of leather-hard clay affords greater freedom in handling the clay. The units with which one builds can be larger, the forms possibly more complex than when one is building with plastic slabs. The loss of plasticity, by the same token, influences the look. The forms tend to be more rigid. Precision, rather than fluidity, is the dominant feature of pieces that exploit the nature of leather-hard clay.

If so desired, the loss of plasticity can be circumvented, to some extent at least, by careful planning. The slabs, for instance, can be undulated, textured or otherwise formed at the plastic stage, allowed to become leather-hard, and then assembled into flowing, organic, or geometric, precise forms.

In building with large building units at the leather-hard stage, one can distinguish between two basic techniques: (1) combining flat leather-hard slabs [111–114], or (2) combining units that have been formed in some manner at the

115

plastic stage [115–119]. In assembling, no real distinction has to be made between the two types. However, in designing the pieces, it is structurally sounder not to think of the leather-hard clay slab as a piece of wood. Whenever a leather-hard slab is used, it should be, if at all possible, curved, even if ever so slightly. This way, it can respond to the stresses of drying and firing by bending.

In assembling the leather-hard slabs and/or forms, it is important to keep two considerations

in mind. (1) All the pieces should be of approximately the same consistency. Because of the shrinkage of clay in drying, mixing leather-hard and plastic slabs will most likely result in cracking and warpage. (2) Proper joining methods are of utmost importance in assembling leather-hard pieces, since, with increased hardness, the probability of the joint holding together in drying and firing decreases. All joints have to be scored and slipped, carefully considering where the slabs meet and where the reinforcement

116

117

118

119

touches the leather-hard clay [111, 115]. Bevel the edges for maximum contact area [118], and insure good contact by pressing the joint together [112, 116, 119] and paddling [113, 117]. Be careful to paddle in the direction that drives the joint together [117].

The joint can be dealt with in a number of ways. It can be left showing, even emphasized, or totally obscured (see joining, p. 35; photo 21).

For a precise look, edges can be worked with woodworking tools, such as a Surform tool [114]; for a softer look, the corners can be rounded by either paddling or scraping [113].

Assembling leather-hard pieces is only one step in the whole process of making a form. There is the preparatory stage, the assembling, and then the refining and enriching stage, where the surface can be textured, substantial changes in form can be achieved by paddling, or several forms or techniques can be combined.

Working with large leather-hard slabs or leather-hard forms which have been previously formed is probably the most commonly used technique of professional ceramicists. It allows one to exploit the plasticity of the clay and the structural strength of leather-hard clay for a great variety of forms, from freely flowing ones to precise, rigidly constructed ones, and from the simple to the very complex.

120

Paddling

Paddling is used frequently to strengthen the joints (see p. 35) and control the texture and surface (see pp. 109, 110; photos 127, 128) of a ceramic piece. It can also play a substantial part in the forming process. Previously formed pieces can be altered substantially by paddling [120] or they can be refined and clarified. Paddling can result in extremely subtle and highly controlled forms, and numerous variations of one basic form are possible [120].

121

122

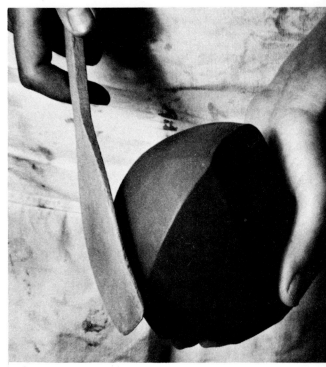

123

124

The form to be paddled can be made by any method and should reflect the basic proportions of the final piece. The extent to which alterations in shape can be made depends in part on the consistency of the clay when it is paddled. Most paddling is done at the soft leather-hard or leather-hard stage. The form in this case moves only where the paddle touches it, which gives one greater control.

It is very important to use the right paddle and to paddle in the correct manner. As discussed under tools (p. 14), it is hard, if not impossible, to find paddles in the tool departments of even the best-equipped ceramic supply houses. Mostly, paddles are adapted from other uses, such as spoons or baseball bats, or they are made by the ceramicist himself or herself.

Paddles usually should be made of wood (because of the absorbency of wood) and should have some weight to them. Depending on the size and shape of the piece to be paddled, different paddles are needed: the larger the piece, the larger the paddle; for a flat side, a flat paddle (with the edges sanded to avoid dents) [121]; for concave curves, a convex paddle, etc. [122].

One paddles from the wrist in short strokes spaced closely together. The paddle should be considered an extension of the hand, feeling its way around a form. It is important to keep the paddle clean (in order to obtain the desired surface density) and dry (or it will stick to the clay). Whenever possible, counteract the pressure from the paddling by supporting the wall on the other side with your hand.

Paddling to me means absolute control of the form: planes can be made to angle just a certain way, ridges can be placed just so [123], and made sharp or tapered. Surfaces can be textured [124].

125

Rims [125] as well as the bottoms [126] can be sculpted.

Gently paddling a totally closed form on one side causes the other to bulge naturally from the force of the air inside.

Though one usually paddles from the outside in, interesting forms can be achieved by paddling from the inside out.

Paddling drives the particles of clay closer together, which seems at times to make the clay wetter. If the clay becomes rubbery, stop and let it dry a bit.

When paddling totally closed forms, one very often decreases the inside volume, so a hole should be provided to allow the excess air to escape.

Paddling is a technique, as far as I know, unique to clay. Wood, plaster, and stone have to be sanded, scraped, and carved, but clay will move under my paddle to where I want it, with a minimum of effort.

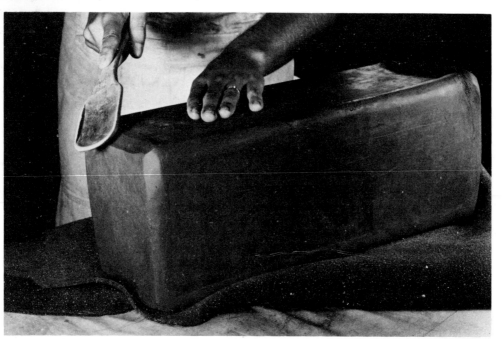

126

6
Surface Treatment

The surface of an unglazed piece of ceramics betrays, often more than the form, the amount of experience of its maker. This is due not just to the attention to detail in general of the experienced professional, but more to the responsiveness of clay, as mentioned earlier. In this chapter, I will concern myself with three aspects of surface treatment. I will discuss ways to retain the fresh, clean look of the clay; suggest ways to regain control over the surface; and outline the most common ways of texturing clay surfaces. These methods are limited to the treatment of clay surfaces at the plastic and leather-hard stages, and represent only one aspect of all the possible surface treatments of ceramic forms. Glazing, staining, and the different firing methods also affect the surfaces of ceramic forms and have a profound effect on their feel and appearance. Discussions of these processes are, however, beyond the scope of this book, and I refer you to the Bibliographical Note for detailed information.

Retaining a Fresh Surface

To retain the fresh look of clay, certain basic precautions must be taken. One is a matter of simple housekeeping: tools—in particular, paddles—and the working surface should be free of dried clay or any other kind of dirt. A slab of clay beaten out over a smooth and clean cloth will have that dense, fresh look that is so particular to clay, but just a few dried-up pieces of clay will ruin that look.

The major cause, however, for losing the fresh look of clay, at least for beginners, is excessive and often unnecessary handling of the plastic clay, and handling it without an awareness of its responsiveness. Every time you touch plastic clay, it shows. It is equivalent to touching a sheet of white paper with a black marker. Discipline and developing that special touch are the keys.

Regaining Control over the Surface

Handling, however, often cannot be avoided, and the question then is how one can regain the fresh look of clay. The answer is that one cannot. You cannot regain that untouched virginal look, but you can achieve a dense and controlled surface. I use paddling for this purpose, since it achieves a hard surface by driving the particles closer together at the same time as it refines the shape. The wetter the clay is when you paddle, the smoother the surface will get. And you can achieve what appears to be a controlled surface with some variation in depth when paddling all the high points of the surface so that they are on one level, while leaving indentations [127, 128].

Scraping with a metal rib or wooden modeling tool is another way. It removes any unevenness but sometimes, particularly when the scraping is done at the leather-hard stage, reveals the grog

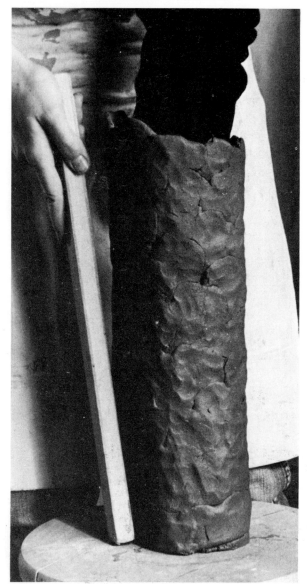

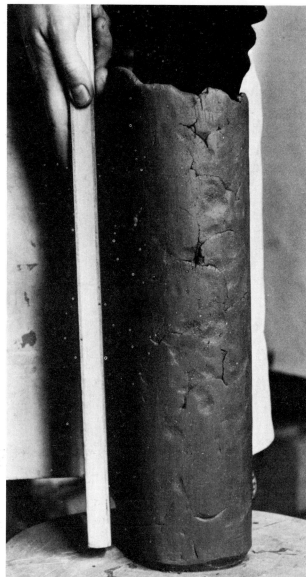

127   128

in the clay. If you move in the direction of the flow of the form when scraping, this can enhance the form with the slight texture it may leave.

Going over the surface with a sponge, or evening out the surface by rubbing it with one's finger or hand, should be done with great care. One has to be careful not to wash away the fine particles of clay or just gloss over bumps and dents. In general, smooth and controlled surfaces can be achieved by a combination of scraping and paddling.

Timing is another important factor when trying to rejuvenate the surface. No firm rule can be established, but I have found that it is best done at the leather-hard stage when the clay has lost some of its responsiveness, yet still retains some of its plasticity.

Texturing

The responsiveness of clay becomes particularly apparent when one thinks of texturing. The plasticity of clay makes it possible to give it the hard look of metal, the softness of fabric, fur, or leather, the thorniness of thistles, or the sensuousness of skin. Textures made with clay can range from the most rugged and jagged to the most subtle and delicate.

Both plastic and leather-hard clay can be textured, although some methods may be more appropriate for one than for the other. Results of the same texturing method when applied to either the plastic or the leather-hard clay may be quite different.

Methods of texturing clay fall into three categories: (1) taking away clay; (2) adding clay; and (3) neither adding nor taking away, but changing the level of the surface by impressing and indenting. This last is particularly appropriate for clay.

Clay can be carved with a minimum of effort both at the plastic and at the leather-hard stage [129]. Almost any tool, such as a modeling tool,

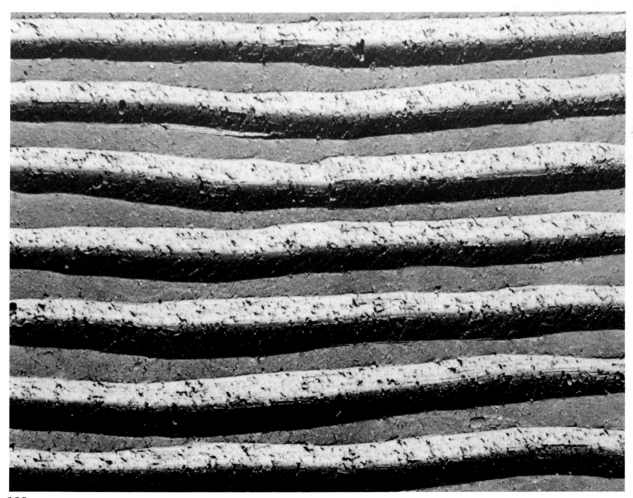

129

130

trimming tool, or knife, may be used [130]. Leather-hard clay can be carved with more precision than plastic clay, yet neither stage allows the precision of wood carving, a fact that can be an advantage. When carving clay, one has to consider the structural consequences of taking clay away and possibly creating weak spots.

Scraping the top layer of fine clay to reveal the grog is another way of texturing that falls into this category and is particularly effective with a heavily grogged clay at the leather-hard stage. The direction in which one scrapes will influence the way one perceives the flow of the form [131].

The surface of a form or slab can be enriched by adding clay to it [132–135]. This can be done with the clay of the slab or form at the leather-hard or plastic stage. In adding plastic clay to leather-hard clay, you must consider the different amount of shrinkage. Scoring and slipping have to be done in such a way as not to interfere with the look of the texture.

When the contact area is small, I dampen the clay even when adding plastic to plastic clay. Wherever possible, increase the contact area by firmly pushing the clay down. Coils or dots of clay that just sit on top of the clay tend to fall off once the piece is dry. Therefore, I design my textures so that they allow me to smooth down at least one side of the added clay [132].

131

132

133

Clay can be added in very tiny amounts to give a hairy look [133], smeared on freely [134], or added in long orderly ridges [132]. One can inlay different-colored clays, or clay of the same color but a slightly harder consistency, by simply rolling the clay into the slab with a rolling pin [135].

The methods that change the surface by indenting and impressing clay at the plastic stage [136–141] exploit the plasticity of the clay most effectively. This can be done in numerous ways. Clay can be indented with a tool [136]; with

134

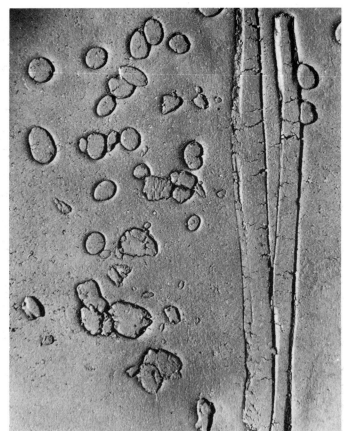

135

136

137

138

139

140

pieces of wood, such as clothespins [137] or slats [138]; with stamps [139]; or with rollers [140]. The last two can be made of wood, or clay that is fired to bisque temperature, or by carving blocks of plaster. In fact, designs with raised fine lines are best done with stamps or rollers. Finely textured cloth, elaborate lace, or rough burlap may be rolled onto the slab to transfer its texture (see pp. 197, 198; photos 237, 238) .

141

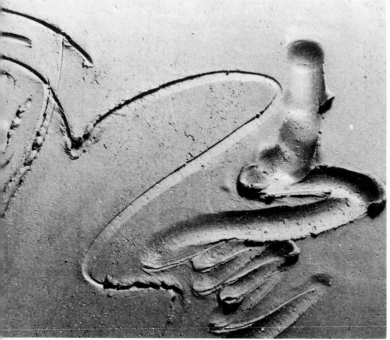

142

Grooves and protrusions can be made in the same motion, either with tools [141] or with fingers.

Whenever one textures a clay surface, one has to consider the condition of the surface prior to texturing. It is difficult to obscure a tired surface with texturing, and it is usually best to establish a smooth, clean surface first. One also has to consider what one is texturing: the type of clay body has a profound influence on the texture. Smooth, very plastic clays will produce different textures than will rough, heavily grogged ones.

In general, when one textures, one manipulates the light. One creates indentations and ridges which make shadows and catch the light. The same texture looks different if it is applied in a different direction. Sometimes if one bends a textured slab slightly, this brings out the texture more sharply.

When texturing, one almost always repeats a certain unit (a thumbprint or toolmark). The spacing and rhythm between these units is crucial. If they are spaced too far apart and too scattered, the eye does not see them as a group but as individual units. Experimentation will tell you when the spacing is right. Because clay lends itself so beautifully to texturing, it can easily be overdone. Texture should enhance the form, not obliterate it. Restraint is often a good tool.

Although there is a difference between texture and image, the same methods used in texturing can be used to create an image on clay. A plastic clay slab, for instance, lends itself beautifully to drawing. The clay shows every change in pressure, not only by the thickness of the line but also by the depth of it. The ridge that is created as it is incised further enriches the line and adds a new dimension [142].

To sum up: The integration of form and surface is of utmost importance for any piece. The responsiveness of clay and its plasticity are manifested not only in the forms but also in the surface. The importance of choosing the right surface for one's forms and paying close attention to the quality of the surface cannot be stressed enough, since it is the surface that is the skin that reveals the form.

7
Specific Forms

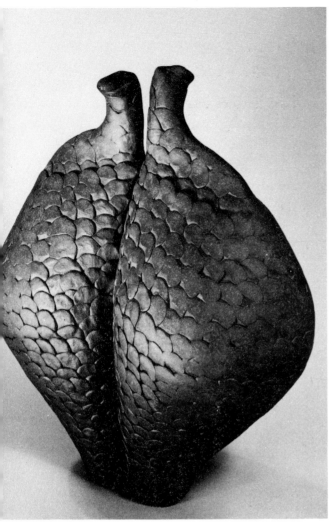

Richard Thomas, stoneware jar. 24" × 24"
Method: extended pinch method

Basic Shapes

Cylindrical forms can be made with almost any process. If a texture or pattern is desired on the outside, the method of joining many small units creates the form and texture at the same time. For smooth cylindrical forms of relatively small size, I would use a plastic slab wrapped around a cardboard tube. For large cylindrical forms, the small-unit method, and in particular the extended pinch method, may be best.

Small *cup-like forms* can be made with the pinch method. Stems can be added by bending a slab into a tubular form.

Slightly curved, plate-like, or *almost flat* forms are best made with a plastic slab, using a hump mold, press mold, or hammock.

Box forms are also best done with slabs; small ones with plastic slabs, large ones with leather-hard slabs. You can texture the surface either before assembling the slabs or afterwards. The extended pinch method can also be used. Paddling the form at the leather-hard stage can produce very precise corners.

Spherical and *elliptical forms* are among the most difficult to achieve. They can be made by joining two forms made with drape or press molds. The methods of building with small units may also be used, for which you must start with a very small bottom and work in numerous stages.

For *bowl-like* pots, one can start with a round bottom made in a press or drape mold and then continue with the small-unit methods.

The preceding chapters in this first part of the book have concerned themselves with the different processes of making ceramic forms. In order to keep the emphasis on the process, the discussions deliberately neglected mention of particular products.

This chapter will summarize what processes are best used for particular types of forms. Methods of making lidded forms are also discussed, and I will point out the important considerations in making composite and large-scale forms.

Paul Soldner

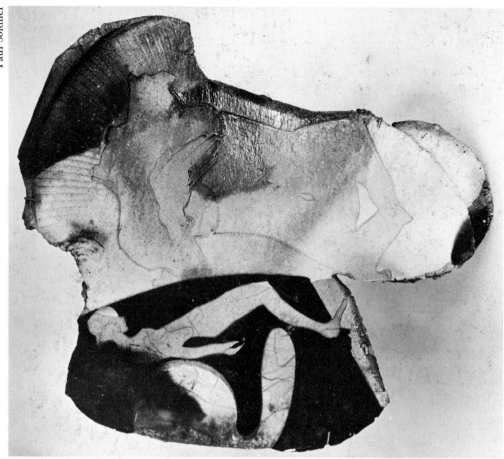

Paul Soldner, raku plaque. 22″ × 18″
Method: slab

Sema Kamrass, raku plate. 20″ in diame
Method: slab-built over a hump mold

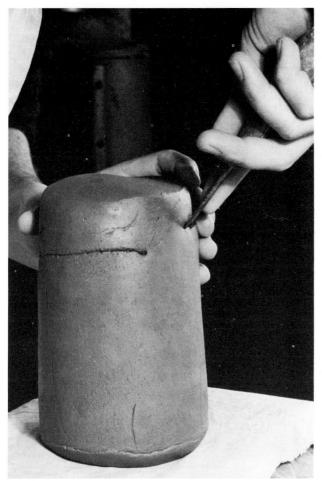

143

144

Lidded Forms

Lidded forms may present special problems, but thinking of them in terms of two interlocking forms simplifies matters. It is important that the two forms fit together well, with the top form secured to the bottom form in some manner to keep it from falling off when the form is tilted. In addition, lid and container should form a visual unit.

Among the many possibilities, there are two simple ways to fulfill these requirements: (1) one can make the lid and the container as one and cut the lid off [143–147], or the container can be finished first and the lid continued on the container or fitted to the container [148–151].

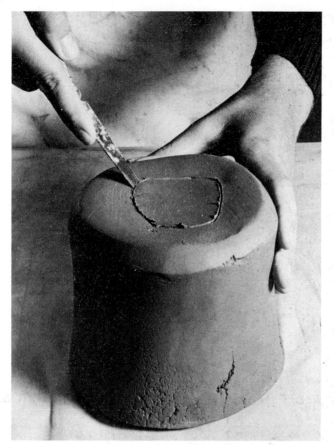

145

146

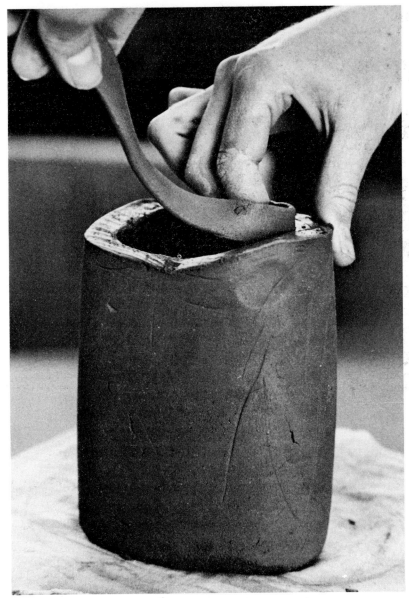

147

In the first instance, a form is made totally closed and the lid cut out usually at the leather-hard stage [143, 145]. If the knife is held at an angle while cutting, the slant of the edge is usually sufficient to keep the cover in place [144]. Pull the knife through in one movement, like a knife through butter. If you saw back and forth with the knife, the cut edge will be very rough.

It is always helpful to run a damp sponge over the cut edge to round it off.

A totally closed form can also be cut with a wire [146]. Since this results in a horizontal cut, it is usually necessary to attach a ribbon of clay on the inside that keeps the lid in place [147]. Partially overlap the ribbon with the top edge of the container, and smooth the clay down on

148

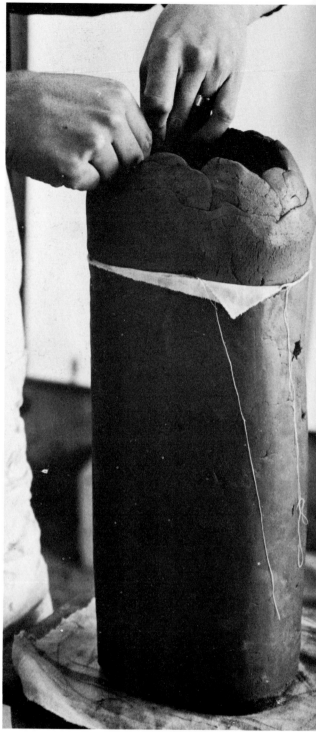

149

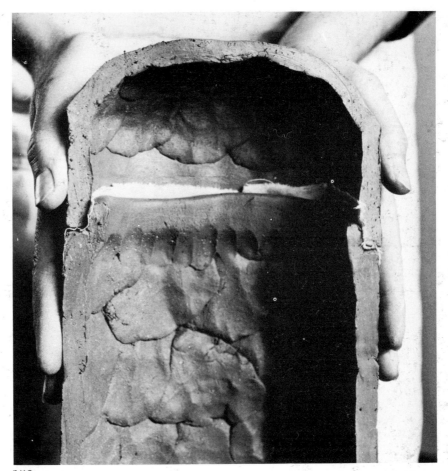

150

the inside. Slightly tilt the top edge of the ribbon inward, so it does not bind with the cover.

The advantage of making containers with covers from totally closed forms is that the lid will always fit exactly, visually as well as technically. The cut separating the lid and the container can follow the form and design of the piece and thus be an integral part of it.

The second way of making lidded forms is to form the container first and then either build the lid on top of it or fit it on later.

In the first instance, the container of the form is finished; a ribbon is attached to the inside of the top edge to keep the cover in place. Then the top is started directly on the rim of the container with a layer of cloth as a separator [148]. The container and the lid can then be thought of as one and finished together [149, 150].

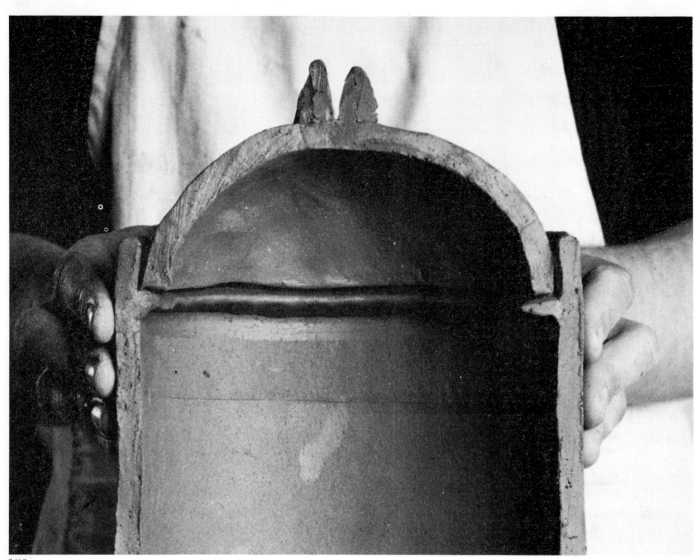

151

Another way to secure a lid to the container is to form a seat on the inside of the container for the lid to sit on [151], by attaching a triangular-shaped coil to the inside. The cover can be formed separately and made to fit or built directly on the seat. Make sure that the seat is wider than necessary, for extra shrinkage, and that the seat is far enough down in the container so that the edge can hold the cover in place. To secure the seat firmly to the container, I usually work in a reinforcing coil underneath it.

Numerous combinations and variations of these two ways to make lidded forms are possible. In addition, different types of handles can alter the look of a piece radically. It is a revealing exercise to make a container with different kinds of lids, to see the change in feeling and expression of the piece as you change the form of the lid or handle. There are, however, some considerations that must be taken into account with all types of lids. They relate to the shrinkage of the clay.

It is crucial that the lid and container be made from clay that is of the same consistency. Do not make the container, let it become leather-hard, and then make the lid out of plastic clay. If you do have to make the lid and the container at different times, take the measurement for the lid when the container is at the plastic stage.

Lid and container are almost always allowed to dry fitted together and are usually fired as one piece.

Whatever acts as the seat for the cover should be made sufficiently wide. Even if one uses clay of the same consistency, the shape may influence the rate of shrinkage. The cover may shrink slightly more or slightly less than the container, and you should allow for this possibility when designing the seat.

Composite Forms

Composite forms are among the most difficult to make, both from the aesthetic and from the technical point of view. Aesthetically, it is hard to combine different forms into a cohesive whole.

The technical difficulties of keeping the pieces together all stem from the fact that clay shrinks as it dries. The solutions to the technical difficulties lie thus in procedures that minimize or eliminate the stresses caused by shrinkage, and are related also to the size of the contact area and the type of joint used, as well as the timing of joining.

If a composite form that touches a plane at several points is placed on a clay slab, the stress between the forms is totally eliminated, since the clay slab moves the forms together as they and the slab shrink. The forms should not be attached to the slab, so they can be removed after the firing (see p. 39; photo 24).

The contact area between the forms should be as large as possible, and the forms, whenever possible, should interlock rather than just touch (see Nicholas, pp. 173, 174).

The timing of joining the forms is another crucial factor. The forms must be stiff enough to be handled and support their own weight, yet the harder the clay becomes, the less likely that a joint will survive. That is, join the forms as soon as possible. As always, the forms should be of the same consistency, to avoid uneven shrinkage. If supports are needed, use clay or materials that take the shrinkage of the clay into account.

Also, be careful not to trap air when joining the forms. Provide for a continuous airflow from one form to the other and to the outside.

Slow and even drying is essential, following the procedures outlined on p. 42 ff.

None of the above concerns is specific to composite forms, but composite forms allow for far less latitude in following these procedures than do other, more simple forms.

Large~Scale Works

Ceramics is rarely thought of in terms of large- and architectural-size pieces. Because of the apparent softness of the material at the plastic stage and its brittleness at the bone-dry stage, sculptors have a hard time imagining the use of it for large-scale works. However, clay is just as suitable a material for large works as any other. It even offers a number of advantages, such as the relative low cost of the material, and its durability, not to mention the enormous expressive potential of clay and the ease of the various hand-building techniques. It is not necessary to acquire new skills to work on a large scale. Any of the forming methods is suitable, and in particular the method of using small units. It is essential, however, to consider the maxims of clay most carefully—in particular, the problems that shrinkage might cause, and the lack of structural strength of clay at the plastic stage. Slow and even drying and the use of a clay body that is open and has a low percentage of shrinkage are prerequisites for the successful completion of a work.

Large works may be approached two ways. One can work in singular monolithic structures, or one can break up the work into small sections that interlock or stand next to each other.

Monolithic Structures

When one works with monolithic structures, the lack of structural strength of clay at the plastic stage and the brittleness of the bone-dry clay, plus the weight, are problems that call for particular attention. The problems created by the lack of structural strength of plastic clay can be solved by working in stages, by building in an interior webbing, and, if necessary, by using a support system. One should remember, however, that clay is quite strong at the leather-hard stage and can support its own weight remarkably well. I do not know what the limit is but I have built pieces more than eight feet tall and about one half inch thick that didn't buckle.

The brittleness of the bone-dry form becomes a problem when the piece has to be put into the kiln. This is easily circumvented by building the form on a piece of plywood three-quarters of an inch thick and lifting the piece into the kiln with the plywood (see pp. 208, 211; photo 253). There is no need then to handle the piece itself. The wood will burn out or turn to charcoal. (Unfortunately, this cannot be done in an electric kiln.)

The problem of weight is minimized if the piece is built on a dolly, so that it never needs to be lifted.

To work with large monolithic forms, it is necessary to have available equally large kilns. When this is not the case, one must turn to the second approach, that of working in sections or multiples.

Sections

Working in sections can be approached in three ways. (1) A large piece is built as one unit and then cut into parts at the leather-hard stage. These parts are then reassembled after the piece has been fired. (2) The piece is built in separate, self-supporting units that interlock; or (3) multiples are used.

The first approach can create severe problems, not only in the handling of the fragile pieces but also in that it can cause warpage because the units lack reinforcement. For this reason, I will discuss only the second and third approaches.

The second way of working in separate, self-supporting, hollow sections requires, above all, careful planning. It is necessary first to spell out what I mean by "separate, self-supporting units." I do not necessarily mean that each section has to be a form with sides, bottom, and a top. I do

David Shelly

Jim Stephenson, Large Brick Clay Wall. 9′ × 32′
Method: two-piece mold

mean, however, that each section can stand by itself. This can mean, for instance, that a tubular form, instead of having a bottom and top, has a ring on the inside, both on the bottom and on the top. This ring reinforces the edge and keeps it from warping. It also provides a larger contact area than just the rim would supply, either for later gluing or to provide a wider seat, should one unit shrink more than the other.

Most important is the system of interlocking the pieces. Pieces that stack on top of each other are much more easily constructed than pieces that interlock sideways. For the first type, I follow the principles outlined under lidded forms—especially the method whereby the lid is built right on the rim of the container (see pp. 126, 127; photos 148–150). This allows me to build the pieces on top of each other and disassemble them for the firing once they are completed.

When building pieces that interlock sideways, you have to take into account that the shrinkage of the clay, rather than drawing the forms closer together, separates them. This makes it very difficult to keep the forms in their proper relationship to each other, and it is therefore advisable, if possible, to build the pieces separately and interlock them at the leather-hard stage.

No matter what method is used to interlock the forms, all sections should be kept at the same consistency as much as possible and dried evenly.

Since the seam or gap between the sections can rarely be totally obscured, it is usually better to work those joints into the design of the piece.

Another option that can enlarge your repertoire of large-scale works is that of building sections either upside down or sideways. Depending on the size of the sections, they can be put right side up when leather-hard or fired in the position they have been built in.

Working in sections can be very exciting. Careful planning and handling, as well as taking the precaution of carefully measuring each section before it dries, so it can be replaced if necessary, are essential.

The third approach, that of using multiples, is discussed in detail in the second part of this book, p. 203 ff.

Large, architectural pieces are very often thought of as outdoor pieces, which raises the question of the durability of the fired clay. Water should not affect any properly fired piece of ceramics. In regions where the temperature drops below freezing, pieces fired to earthenware temperatures cannot be kept outside, since earthenware clay is usually still water-absorbent. When the water freezes, the clay is pulled apart. Properly fired stoneware, however, can withstand most winter climates, as long as water cannot collect inside the form.

8

Handbuilding with Wheelthrown Forms

The technique of wheelthrowing cannot be explained in one chapter and, as I have mentioned before, it is treated thoroughly in my book *Pottery on the Wheel*. For those readers who have wheelthrowing skills or intend to acquire them, it may be useful to point out some of the possibilities of handbuilding with wheelthrown forms. These fall generally into three categories: altering the wheelthrown form; combining wheelthrown parts with handbuilt parts; combining several wheelthrown forms, either whole or sections thereof.

It is important to note that these categories do not employ new handbuilding techniques but simply present new variations of the now very familiar techniques. Therefore, all the rules and procedures of joining, wall thickness, drying, etc., apply as much to these methods as they do to the other forming methods. The wheelthrown part should be thought of as a building unit— usually a large one, and more often than not at the leather-hard stage, since the freshly thrown pot is too fragile to be handled.

Altering the Wheelthrown Form

My favorite way of altering a wheelthrown shape is paddling. As with any handbuilt form, paddling is best done when the clay is leather-hard and the form trimmed. The perpetually round, symmetrical form of wheelthrown work can be quickly changed by this method into a great variety of diverse forms. Texturing and distorting the form immediately after throwing are other possibilities that fall into this category.

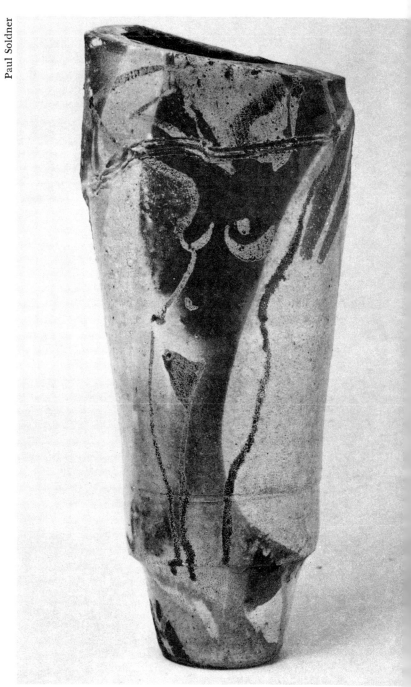

Paul Soldner

Paul Soldner, raku vase. 18" × 6"
Method: wheelthrown, then turned upside down

Jean-Pierre Beaudin

Hélène Gagné, stoneware vase. 19" × 14"
Method: alternating wheelthrown parts with coils flattened by paddling

Penny Hood Hoagland, porcelain vase. 6.5" × 6.5"
Method: bottom wheelthrown, then continued with coils

Combining Wheelthrown Parts with Handbuilt Parts

Combining wheelthrown with handbuilt parts offers a wide variety of possibilities. One can start with a thrown form and continue with handbuilding, particularly with small units such as coils. A handbuilt form can also be topped off with a thrown section. Thrown and handbuilt parts can alternate with each other in successive layers, etc. The proportion of handbuilt to thrown parts can vary a great deal, from the attachment of a few protrusions to the wheelthrown form to the building of a piece that almost obliterates the thrown aspects. The transition from one part to the other may be deliberately abrupt or gradual.

It is important to keep in mind the consistency of the clays that are joined. Because of its fragility, the thrown part is mostly used at the leather-hard stage, and if leather-hard and plastic units are to be mixed, careful consideration should be given to the stresses this might set up. Careful joining and slow drying are essential.

Jean-Pierre Beaudin

Hélène Gagné, The Butterfly. Stoneware. 34″ × 26″ × 8″
Method: assembled thrown parts

Combining Several Wheelthrown Parts

When combining several wheelthrown forms, keep in mind the same considerations and rules as when working with large leather-hard forms—especially those outlined earlier under "Composite Forms." One can combine entire forms or sections cut from thrown shapes. The forms can interlock with each other, be stacked on top of each other, or stand side by side. Thorough scoring and slipping, large contact area, and reinforcement of the joints are essential. Paddling may be used both to adjust the forms to each

Elsbeth S. Woody, Arch. Stoneware. 5' × 7' × 2'
Method: (center) combined wheelthrown parts; (arms) extended pinch method

other and to insure a smooth and gradual transition where one wants it, as well as to strengthen the joints.

Thrown parts can be combined in such a manner that each part retains its integrity as a finished form, or they may flow into each other, losing their individuality for the sake of the total form.

Although the methods of handbuilding with wheelthrown shapes do not constitute new handbuilding techniques as such, the forms that result have certain discernible common qualities that are quite unique. They often combine the symmetry and fullness of wheelthrown forms with the variety and diversity of handbuilt forms.

TEN APPROACHES TO HANDBUILDING

Part One of *Handbuilding Ceramic Forms* covers the various techniques of making forms with clay. The emphasis is on the processes and procedures. A deliberate effort was made to avoid distracting the reader by showing specific products.

Part Two, on the other hand, will show how professional ceramicists use, vary, and combine the techniques discussed earlier.

For each ceramicist, I will show from beginning to end the important steps in creating a particular piece, as well as other examples of the artist's work. The intent is both to show the application of the techniques and also, and perhaps most important, to give the reader a sense of the sequence a work goes through, from the conception of an idea to the finished product. The emphasis will be on the variety of approaches of the artists to their material, as well as on the technique involved.

It is hoped that this shift in emphasis from the process to the product will not result in mere copying but will inspire the reader to search for expression in clay that is uniquely his or her own.

Much had to be left out. The choice of the artists and the works was guided by a desire to show the greatest diversity in techniques. It should in no way be considered a survey of the styles and trends of contemporary ceramic art.

Elaine Katzer, Whitney's Wall. Stoneware. 8.5' × 11'

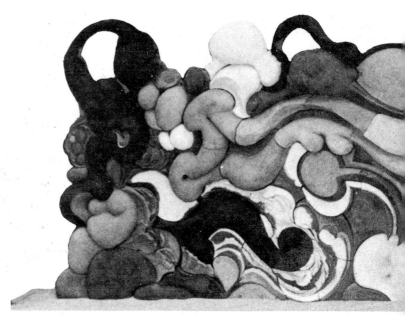

Elaine Katzer, Sea Chanty. Stoneware. 7' × 22'

ELAINE KATZER

Building large ceramic murals can present many problems. Usually, ceramicists build them on the floor or on a large easel, and, what is more important, in one solid unit. When the whole piece is finished, it is then cut into sections for drying and firing. If the relief is high, each section has to be hollowed out from the back before the clay becomes too hard.

To build in this manner not only necessitates a large studio but restrictions on the depth of the relief, since the forms are initially solids.

Elaine Katzer has eliminated these major problems. Rather than building the whole piece as one unit and cutting it into manageable sections, Elaine Katzer builds each section as a self-enclosed form that interlocks with the others

Elaine Katzer

[152]. And each section is built as a hollow form; the back is firmly attached to the easel, and Katzer builds out from it, using the extended pinch method [153]. The problem of size has been eliminated by the artist's development of a special easel with movable panels that allows her to build an 8′ high relief of any length in her 17′ × 17′ studio [162] (see p. 150).

152

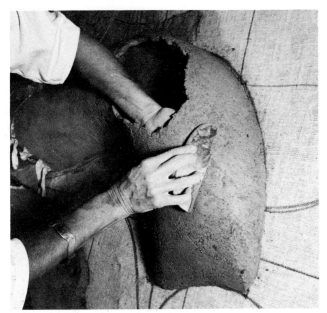

153

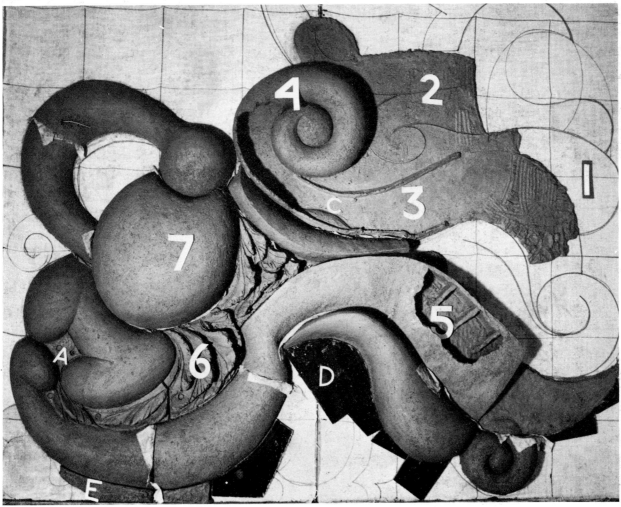

154

155

In addition, she has devised a type of attachment to fix the finished ceramic pieces to the permanent installation site that is in most cases hidden from view [157].

In constructing her wall pieces, Katzer goes through the following procedure:

She works out the design and color pattern on paper, in some cases making a small clay model to determine the highs and lows of the relief.

The drawing is then overlaid with a one-inch grid pattern, and the length of the relief is divided into four-foot units (four inches on the drawing).

Burlap is attached to the panels on the easel and a one-foot grid pattern drawn on it. The burlap is stapled onto the easel in the corners and the center of each one-foot square. With the help of the grid pattern, the design is then drawn on the burlap [155, 154-1]. The sections are built from left to right and from the bottom up. To build the sections, a ½″ thick layer of clay is pounded into the burlap, covering a few square feet. The clay and burlap have to interlock firmly, since this layer of clay will be the back of the forms and the bond between the burlap and the clay must hold the forms to the easel. A ledge at the bottom of the easel helps to support the clay vertically.

The outlines of the sections are then redrawn on the clay [156, 154-2]. Each section is outlined with a coil [154-3], from which the section is built up and totally closed, using the extended pinch method. The section is built in place on the easel as a totally self-enclosed hollow form. Elaine Katzer refines the form and the texture by going over it repeatedly with a large flexible scraper.

156

157

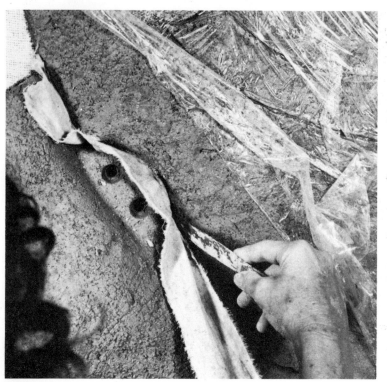

158

159

After each section is finished, the flange is made by which the section is screwed to the wall during the installation of the finished piece. A small area on the edge of the section is thickened, and two holes are made. For each hole, a dowel pierces the entire thickness of the clay after a larger dowel has been pushed only partway through to make room for the screws to be countersunk into the clay. The section with the flange is then cut away from the back of the next section [157], and a strip of cloth is pushed in to make the separation permanent [158]. The cloth also covers the flange. The flange is then covered with a slab of clay that is attached to the back of the next section [159, 161]. This next section is then started again with a coil and is built right over the flange. The flange, then, tucks under the adjoining section [160, 161, 154-C].

The size and position of the flange depend on the size and position of the section. It has to carry the weight and hold the form in place.

Katzer pinches in all directions: up, down, sideways, either squatting, standing, or on a ladder, as the sections demand. The larger sections have to be built in stages, and some need interior braces to hold their shape at the plastic stage [154-5]. The size of each section is determined by the design itself, as well as by the size of the kiln shelf. Large sweeping forms may have to be broken up into several sections, but each section is built as a self-enclosed unit and is separated from the adjoining one with a cloth.

160

Quite often, Katzer incorporates flat areas that have ridges or tentacle-like protrusions attached to them. She makes the back of these parts at least three-quarters to one inch thick [154-6].

If there is a vignette-shaped bottom edge, plywood boards are cut to fit the outline of the bottom edge and are nailed directly to the easel [154-D]. These boards provide the same support as the ledge does at the bottom of the easel. Clay supports starting from the ledge can serve the same function [154-E]. It is important to keep all the pieces on the easel at the same consistency. Sections that are not being worked on are therefore covered with plastic to avoid their drying out.

161

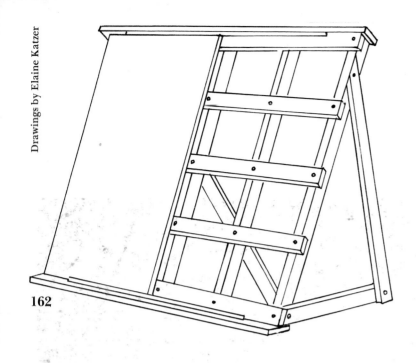

Drawings by Elaine Katzer

162

To overcome the limitations of her small studio, Katzer has devised an ingenious system of movable panels. Each sketch is divided lengthwise into four-foot-wide units and labeled A, B, C, etc. Katzer then draws the designs for units A and B on the burlap [163-1], completes all the forms on A, and starts to build B [163-2]. A and those sections that reach from A into B are removed; the left-hand panel (that is, the one that had A on it) is then removed, and the right-hand panel (that is, the one with B on it) is moved to the left, with the remaining sections of B on it. The panel that has been removed is placed where B was, and C is drawn on it [163-3]. B and part of C are completed [163-4], B removed, C moved to the left, and B becomes D, etc.

This system not only allows reliefs of enormous length to be built but also assures the smooth flow of forms from one unit to the other.

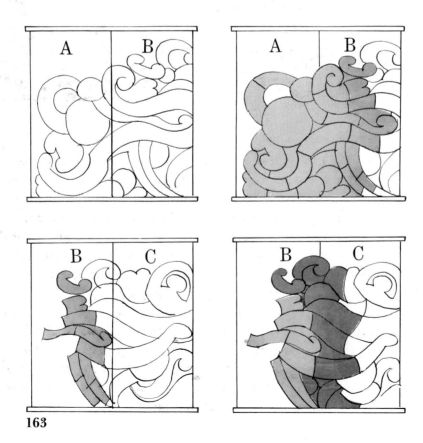

163

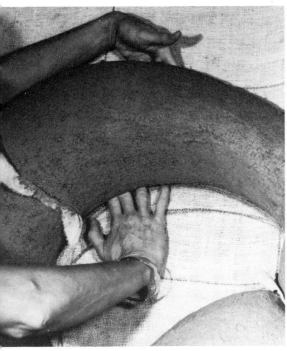

164

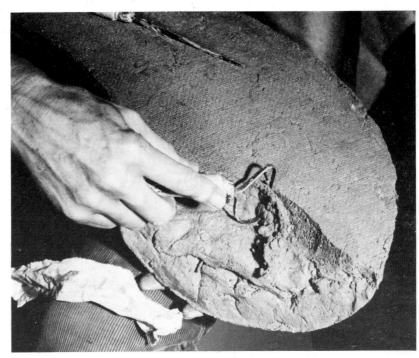

165

The timing of the removal of the sections from the panels is crucial. The forms are allowed to stiffen to the leather-hard stage but have to be removed at the right moment, since the burlap allows only a limited amount of shrinkage. During the drying, the pieces tend to pull off the burlap around the edges, and this space can be used to loosen them entirely [164]. As each section is removed, it is numbered, and an arrow shows which direction is up. This is done on the back, with either white slip or red iron oxide, so that the directions will be fired permanently onto the piece. The number is then recorded on the sketch. All the areas which might come into contact with the flange of an adjoining section are scraped off to allow more room for warpage [165]. Each section is given several air holes in the back, and the holes for the screws are cleaned out. Glazes and slips are applied following the color pattern of Katzer's drawing, and the sections are fired in a reducing atmosphere to about cone 6 (approximately 2100° F.).

Katzer has installed her pieces in a number of locations in California. Usually, she installs several layers of marine plywood to which the pieces are screwed and glued. The fact that most sections weigh less than ten pounds makes their installation much easier.

Elizabeth MacDonald, Nest. Stoneware. 8″ × 12″

Gordon Lewis

ELIZABETH MACDONALD

The work of Elizabeth MacDonald combines extremely simple yet highly sophisticated and beautifully balanced forms with moving and vibrating surfaces that do not easily betray, even to the trained eye, the method by which they were made. Yet MacDonald uses a technique that not only requires a bare minimum of tools but could not be more simple.

For the bottom of her pots, MacDonald uses a slightly curved slab that has been allowed to harden to the leather-hard stage on a hump mold [166]. Using the method of building with small

166

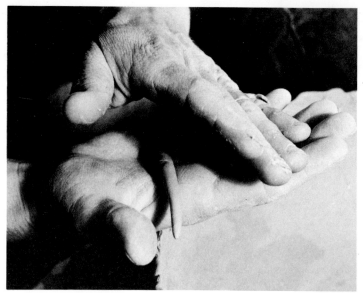

167

168

units, she builds up the form on the slab with short coils, which she quickly rolls out in her hand [167] and attaches very loosely to the ones below, often overlapping them on the outside [168, 169]. After completing a full round, the

169

170

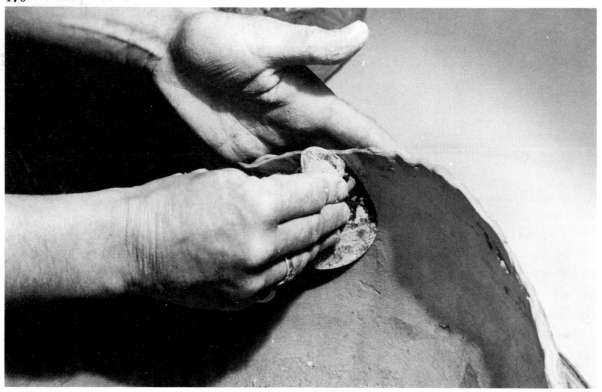

171

coils are smoothed down very carefully on the inside of the pot [170], and any unevenness is scraped off [171]. The outside is then paddled, both to control the form and to help create a special kind of surface [172].

The undulating, vibrating surface results from three factors: the coils are placed so that they slightly overlap each other; the paddling is done in such a way that the coils, rather than being smoothed out, are pushed down into each other in layers; and care is taken not to let the rim become evenly horizontal but instead to keep it rising and falling.

Because the diameter of the form increases rapidly at first and then toward the top begins to decrease, MacDonald has to work in many stages, stopping after every few rounds. Since the wall is only about one-quarter of an inch thick, however, she can resume work after a relatively short time. Instead of scoring and slipping, she sprays the rim with a fine mist of water before resuming her work.

Most of her pieces are glazed on the inside. The glaze is brushed on in a very diluted stage on the outside and rubbed off, so that it remains only in the indentations, thus emphasizing the texture. MacDonald fires the work to stoneware temperatures in an electric kiln.

Texture and form complement each other perfectly in MacDonald's work, with the surface increasing the sense of tension and fullness of the forms, as does the size and shape of the opening. Subtle variations in the relationship of these elements achieve dramatic effects in the visual balance of the pot.

172

Alvin Thompson

David Middlebrook, Dig In. Earthenware. 33″ × 29″ × 15″

DAVID MIDDLEBROOK

David Middlebrook's work, though generally considered part of California Funk, transcends this stylistic categorization for several reasons. Although his imagery, like that of California Funk, contains everyday objects, it lacks the literalness, the sarcastic social comment, and the sometimes considerable and always deliberate bad taste of California Funk. It is, in fact, particularly in its combination of images, much more related to surrealism, and according to Middlebrook he was greatly influenced, particularly in the early stages of his career, by Duchamp and the Dada movement.

However, what distinguishes Middlebrook most from California Funk is his concern for sculptural form, and a sense of energy, inventiveness, and experimentation that also characterizes his way of working.

Although not primarily interested in size, Middlebrook has developed techniques that allow him to exploit fully the plasticity of the clay, even on a large scale, without making concessions to the lack of structural strength of plastic clay. Yet Middlebrook has not developed new techniques as such; it is the adaption of techniques, and the limits to which he dares to push them, that make his way of working unique and exciting.

At the same time, he extracts from the clay those special effects necessary to make clay look just like carrots, cacti, bread, or watermelon. He does this with very simple methods and often without resorting to the use of molds.

The discussion of his techniques will center on two aspects: the methods of constructing the basic forms [173–181], and the methods used to achieve some of the special effects [182–187].

Construction

To construct his pieces, Middlebrook uses, with few exceptions, what he calls his "bag technique."

The *bag technique* follows, in general, the principle of the drape-mold technique or that of working with a large plastic slab using an aid. The aid in this case is a sack or bag made from cloth and filled with vermiculite. The vermiculite, aside from being very light in weight, has two distinct advantages. It compacts as it becomes damp; thus, it does not impede the shrinkage of the clay around it. And the bag is flexible, the degree of flexibility depending on how tightly the vermiculite is packed. This gives the clay form structural strength without becoming an obstacle in the forming. The clay forms, then,

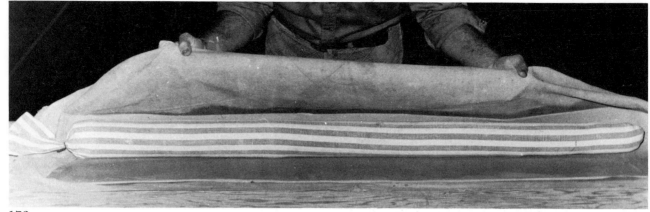

173

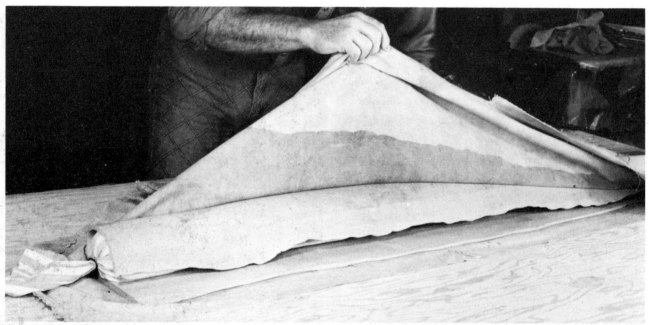

174

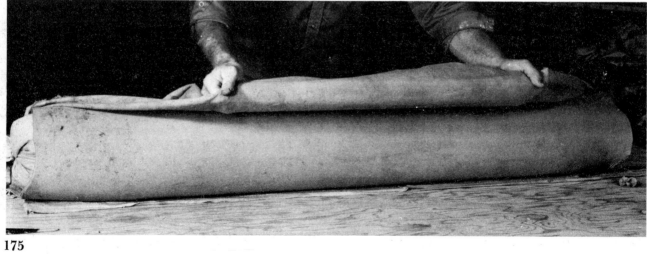

175

can be shaped and reshaped with the bag inside. (This is particularly true when the cloth the sack is made from is of some stretchable material, such as panty hose.)

Middlebrook tends to use the bag or sack for two types of forms. For one type, a long, narrow bag is used to roll a slab around, to create tubular forms [173–180]. For the other, a more mound-like bag is used, over which the clay is draped in the familiar drape-mold fashion [181].

As I have indicated, the bag technique is usually used in conjunction with slabs that are thrown out and, in the case of a very large slab, are joined by overlapping them and then thinning out the whole slab with a rolling pin. The slab is almost always placed on a cloth. It is very important that the cloth be perfectly smooth. Wrinkles form indentations in the clay slab that may become weak spots on the form.

In the case of a tubular form, Middlebrook puts the sack on a slab [173] and pulls the slab around it with the cloth until one edge of the slab touches the rest of the slab [174] and then scores (against the direction of the seam) and slips the joint (even though he is joining plastic to plastic clay). He then continues to roll the form over (again by pulling with the cloth) until the seam is on top [175]. He eliminates all traces of the seam by going over it with a knife and then with a flexible rubber rib, keeping a cloth between the clay and the tool.

For a totally closed form, the ends are squeezed together, with the bag inside.

Not only can tubular forms of tremendous length and diameter be made in this fashion, but these forms can be picked up [176], bent [177], and stood up without fear that they'll collapse [178], dent, or distort. In fact, it is this opportunity to manipulate the forms immediately after the initial construction that makes this process so exciting, particularly since many variations of form are possible with each bag or sack. The variations depend on two factors: the density of the vermiculite in the bag, and how

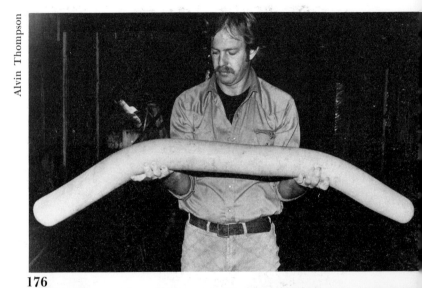

Alvin Thompson

176

Alvin Thompson

177

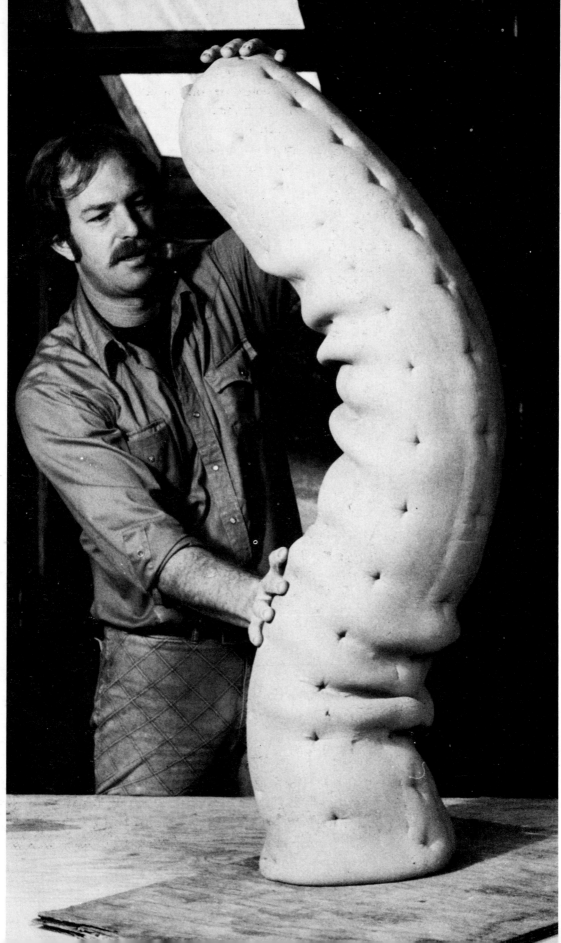

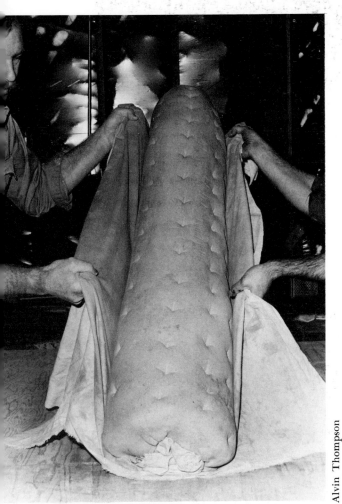

tightly the clay slab is rolled around the bag. The looser the vermiculite in the bag, the more the form can be manipulated. By the same token, the looser one rolls the clay slab around the bag, the softer the form may appear [**178**].

The immediacy, range, and flexibility of this technique open up countless possibilities, from small to large and from soft to rigid forms. However, it may be useful to reiterate some of the precautions one has to take to use this technique successfully. First, make sure there are no wrinkles in the cloth on which the slab is thinned out. Second, whenever possible, do not handle the clay slab or form directly, but use the cloth [**173, 175, 179, 180**]. Third, to avoid denting the forms, lay them on foam rubber. Fourth, if you plan very large forms, you may need several pairs of hands to manipulate them [**179, 180**].

Alvin Thompson

179

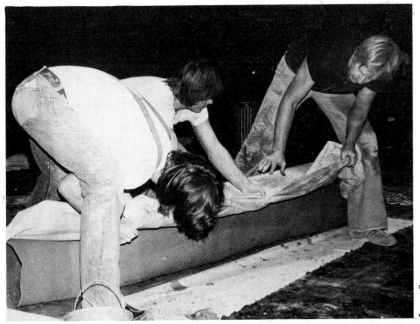

180

Jerry Sawyer

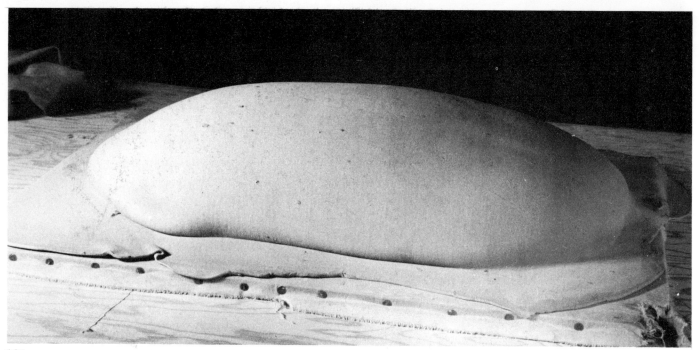

181

The second type of form made possible by the bag is the half-round or mound-like form. The bag may vary in size and shape, and the clay slab is draped over it in the usual drape-mold fashion. What is unique is that Middlebrook uses the drape-mold technique with what he calls a type of vacuum-forming process. This process consists of picking up the whole works (board, bag, and clay slab) and dropping it from a height of one, two, or three feet onto the table or floor. What happens is that the bag bounces and the clay slab is literally sucked under and around the bag form, taking on every detail of the shape of the bag [181]. Rather than pressing the clay slab around the bag with one's hands, one forces the bag into the clay slab (or vice versa), and the clay slab retains the freshness of an untouched surface.

On some of these forms, the slab may be tucked under the form, and eventually, at the leather-hard stage, a bottom may be added [186]. Whenever Middlebrook uses a bag, he almost always leaves the bag inside the clay form until the clay becomes leather-hard, at which point he cuts a hole into the clay and removes the vermiculite with the help of a vacuum cleaner.

Special Effects

Middlebrook's special effects are, with few exceptions, achieved by working directly with the clay rather than relying on molds, and by amazingly simple means. Most of his special effects are achieved through surface treatment, either before or after construction of the form. In the bag technique, most of the surface treatment occurs immediately after the form has been made, with the bag inside the clay form. It is at this stage that Middlebrook incises and indents [182] the clay for a variety of effects [183], such as lines for the carrot, dents for the cactus, etc. The indentations are made on top of at least one layer of cloth that is firmly attached to the clay, using a knife, a pointed tool, the handle of a rolling pin, or even a two-by-four that is hammered into the clay. He uses considerable force, yet is care-

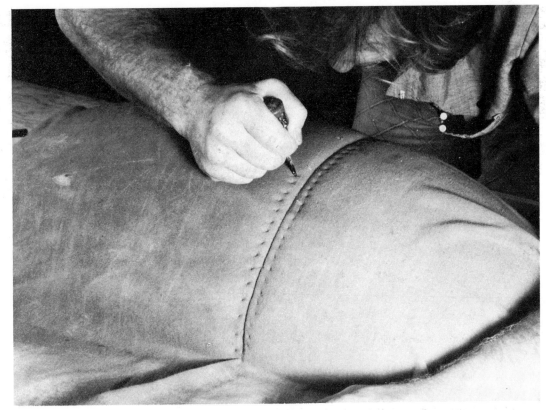

182

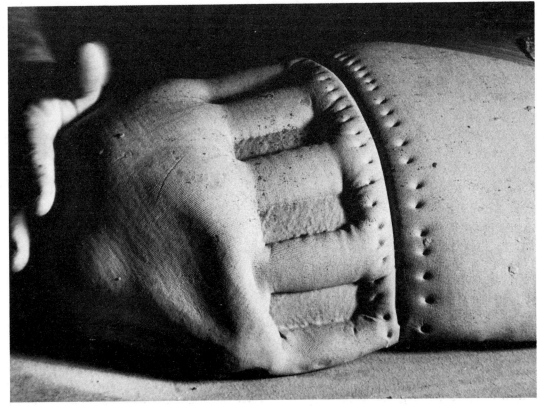

183

184

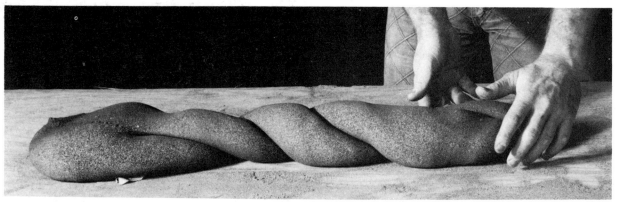

185

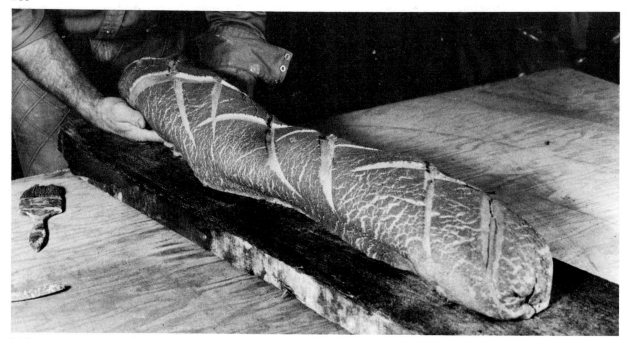

186

ful not to pierce the cloth or the clay, lest that should weaken the form.

By indenting the clay with a cloth firmly rubbed onto the clay (not just lying on top) , one does not thin the clay slab but rather forces it down into the bag, and the clay wall retains the same thickness.

Other special effects, such as the surface of the bread, watermelon, and wood basket, are achieved by texturing the slab before the form is constructed.

The bread texture is made in the following manner. A layer of dry clay powder is rubbed into a thick clay slab, and the slab is incised in a criss-cross pattern [184]. The slab is then thinned to approximately three-eighths of an inch, using the throwing method. This opens up the incisions and creates the effect of the bread crust by breaking open the dry surface of the clay. The slab is then laid over a bag (in this case, panty hose [185]) and vacuum-formed. This results in the typical swelling quality of freshly baked bread [186].

The watermelon is done in a similar fashion, by thinning a slab into which a layer of dry clay has been rubbed. The indentations for the seeds are made after the clay has been thinned, with the slab lying on top of a thick layer of foam, and with a cloth in between the tool and the clay, to avoid piercing the clay. For the stiff slice of watermelon, the form is constructed with the clay slabs at the leather-hard stage; and for the wrinkled, dried-up watermelon, with the slabs at the plastic stage.

The wood textures are made by throwing thin plastic slabs onto a rough piece of wood, once for one side, then turning the wood over for a realistic effect, and throwing the other side of the slab down. The basket form is made by laying these "boards" on a well-packed bag [187]. Staples are added in the form of tiny coils, nails with coils, and tiny flattened balls of clay for the nailhead, hammer indentations with a hammer, etc.

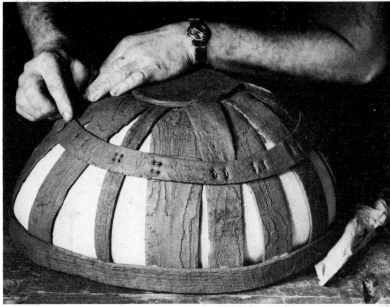

187

Very important to the special effects are the glazes and glazing techniques Middlebrook has developed. A discussion of these techniques is beyond the scope of the book, however, except for the listing of glaze and clay recipes in the Appendix.

The techniques discussed above are just part of the Middlebrook repertoire and represent only part of the entire process. Some of the forms are assembled at the leather-hard stage; others are prepared so that they can be bolted together after the firing. In some cases, the fired clay forms are combined with other materials.

Throughout the construction process, sculptural considerations go hand in hand with the concern for the images. A design may be altered, as the work progresses, both for visual reasons and for reasons of content. It should be stressed that matters of form and content are of uppermost importance to Middlebrook. His expert and daring handling of clay, his inventiveness in regard to technique, and his broad knowledge of general building processes are the foundation upon which his art rests.

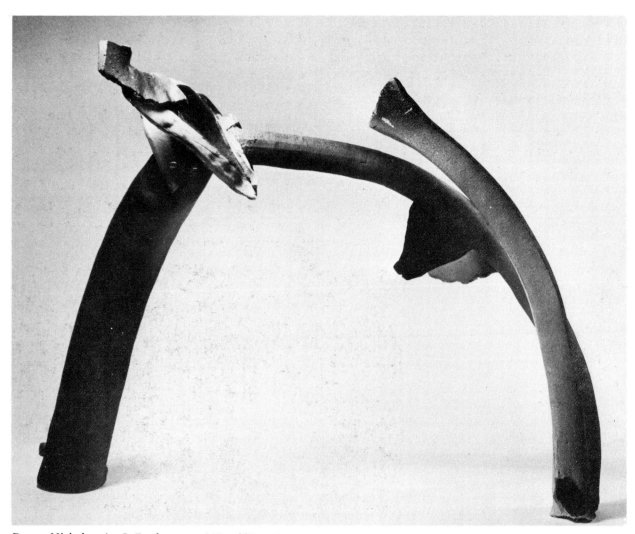

Donna Nicholas, Arc I. Earthenware. 20″ × 33″ × 8″

DONNA NICHOLAS

Donna Nicholas's work combines linear, hard-edged, and organic forms in a complex, yet clearly structured and elegant arrangement. The linear elements set the rhythm of her pieces, while the hard-edged and organic forms give them volume. Yet it is the tension between these forms, the spaces defined and enclosed by them, and the flow of lines from one form to the other, that rivet one's attention, particularly as these relationships change from different viewpoints. The number of these ever changing configurations of forms and spaces is multiplied by the color on the pieces. The colors define the forms as well as draw together different areas from different angles. Color seems to emanate from the forms or grow on the surface like algae or moss on rocks.

The sculptures are assembled from previously constructed forms at the leather-hard stage. The process falls into the four clearly defined phases of planning, preparing the parts, assembling them, and glazing.

Nicholas works out her ideas on paper. The sketch is transferred to scale on large sheets of craft paper, and some sections are cut out to use as patterns for the pieces [188].

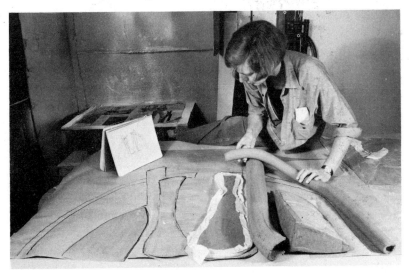

188

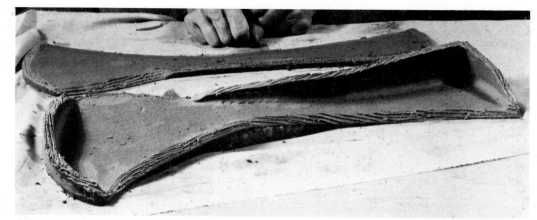

189

190

191

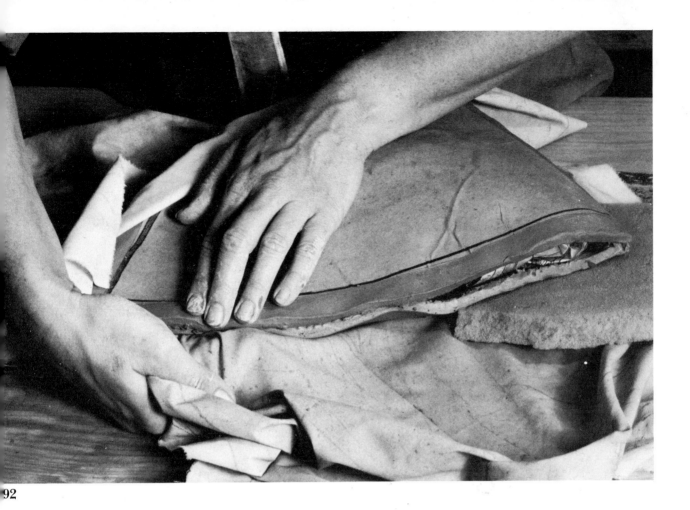

The linear forms are extruded and bent to follow the patterns [188]. The extruded clay contains nylon fibers, which make the tubes both stronger and more flexible.

The hard-edged forms are constructed of leather-hard slabs. The shapes of the slabs have been cut out using the paper patterns. Nicholas wraps the edges of the slabs with plastic, so that they remain softer, for a better joint. Some of the edges of the slabs are beveled according to the angles of the form [189]. Although Nicholas uses leather-hard clay and these forms are basically hard-edged, they are not rigid. Note the foam rubber that supports the curve in the form [190].

The organic forms are also slab-built, but they are made from a combination of plastic and leather-hard clay, in order to achieve softness with the plastic slab and, with the leather-hard slab, retain some rigidity to maintain the form's fullness [191]. Usually, the wide sides are made out of the plastic clay, and the narrow ones out of leather-hard clay. Prior to building the organic forms, the paper pattern is attached to the plastic slab by wetting the slab with a sponge and firmly rubbing the paper onto it. Crumpled newspaper pushed inside the form keeps it from collapsing. In joining the slabs, Nicholas manipulates the clay with the aid of a cloth, pulling the sides together, creating twists and curves, which are then supported with foam rubber [192]. The wrinkles in the forms are created by the paper as the form is twisted. Nicholas does this twisting under the cloth, pull-

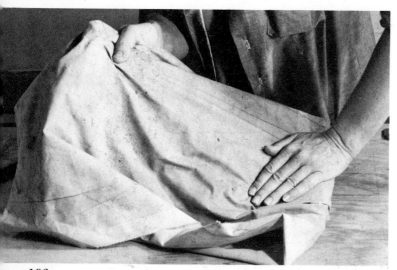

193

194

ing up with one hand and pushing down with the other [193]. The direction of the wrinkles is controlled by the direction in which she twists the form.

Paddling serves both to drive the seams together and to manipulate the clay into its proper shape. Nicholas paddles the form with a cloth over the clay, to keep the paddle from sticking to it and to avoid flattening out the texture [194].

It is interesting to note the manner in which Nicholas manipulates the clay in the forming process. She uses a cloth, not just as a separator, but as a forming tool, pulling sides together and twisting forms with it.

The complexity of this second phase—preparing the parts— warrants a summary to point out the crucial elements. Nicholas prepares three types of forms, each one with a different technique. The linear forms are extruded; the hard-edged and the organic forms are both slab-built, but one with leather-hard slabs, exploiting the structural strength of clay, and the other out of

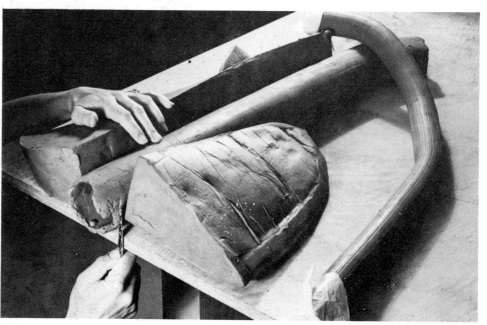

195

a combination of plastic and leather-hard slab (usually a faux pas in ceramics), to exploit the plasticity of clay while taking advantage of the structural strength. The particular way of manipulating the clay with a cloth is uniquely hers and deserves careful observation.

Before the pieces are assembled, they are all allowed to dry to approximately the same leather-hard consistency. It is extremely important that the clay be rigid enough to support its weight, yet flexible enough to allow for alterations of the forms.

The first step in assembling is to establish the groundline. For this purpose, all parts are laid out according to the sketch, along the edge of the table. The tubes are cut accordingly [195], and bottoms are attached to them. All the forms are then equipped with air holes.

Aesthetic as well as technical considerations have to be taken into account in assembling. This is the moment when the two-dimensional sketch is transformed into the three-dimensional construction, and a great deal of time is needed to consider the relationships of the forms from all angles.

On the technical side, all forms have to interlock firmly. Nicholas uses a variety of joints and usually solves the problem slightly differently each time. But certain considerations govern her approach at all times. Whenever possible, she looks for an area of contact, rather than just a point, and for more than one area. She tries to interlock the forms, rather than having them just touch.

The forms may wrap around one another [196]. If two walls meet over a fairly large area, the parts of the walls which meet are usually cut out to lessen the piece's weight, to allow the forms to twist more easily, and so that air can flow from one form to the other, which results in more even drying.

One form may be given a wedge-like protrusion that is inserted into a slot cut into the other [197], or part of one form may be cut out

196

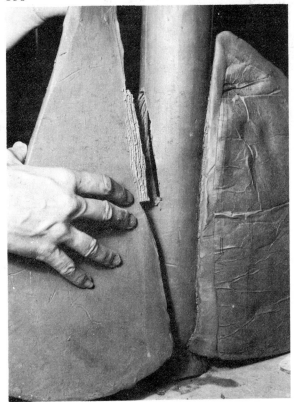

197

198

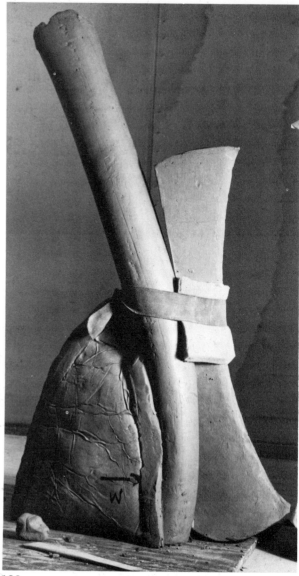

199

so that the other can fit into it [**198**].

All joints are scored, and water is added to them. After the joint is pressed together, a deep groove is made, into which the reinforcing coil is pushed. To pull the forms together, a wide band of elastic is tied around them. The elastic has the advantage that it moves in as the clay shrinks. Again, note the foam rubber for padding [**199**].

During assembling, Nicholas quite often changes the shapes by paddling, cutting away, adding pieces of clay, and twisting the tubes for a different kind of movement. The ends of the tubes may be closed with a slab, torn, or paddled.

The final step in assembling the sculptures is cleaning the joints and refining the surface [**200**]. This is usually done after the piece has been allowed to sit overnight. The time lapse serves two purposes. The wet clay that has been used for reinforcements or to fill gaps has had a chance to harden somewhat; and, more important, Nicholas has had a chance to reevaluate her piece after having gained some distance in time from it.

The sculpture is allowed to dry very slowly, and even though the forms are very complex, Nicholas does not find it necessary to place them on a clay slab. She may, however, fire them on a wooden board to avoid handling the piece in packing the kiln.

In the final phase, the glazing, the color is applied. The color is used in such a way as to rede-fine and emphasize relationships between parts. Nicholas applies the glazes by spraying the bisqued piece, and one piece may go through numerous firings at cone 06 (approximately 1840° F.) and be reglazed over and over again until the desired effects are achieved. Glazing and firing may thus take a great deal longer than constructing the piece.

The technical complexity of the work of Nicholas is matched only by the complexity and richness of her forms. This complexity is coupled with a clarity of design and concept that reflects a logical thought process and careful planning.

200

Sy Shames, stoneware container. 6" × 10"

SY SHAMES

Sy Shames's work is characterized by a simplicity of form, and a surface that is so fresh and full of tension that it seems to be untouched by human hands; the linear pattern and texture seem to be formed accidentally by a natural growing process.

The special kind of surface results from the fact that Shames has perfected the art of throwing out slabs, and that in his method of working he, in fact, rarely touches the outside of his forms. The secret lies in his working almost entirely from the wrong side.

The subtlety of the lines also comes from his particular method of working from the wrong side. After throwing out a large slab and carrying it to the table flat against his body [201] to avoid distorting it, Shames cuts strips off the

201

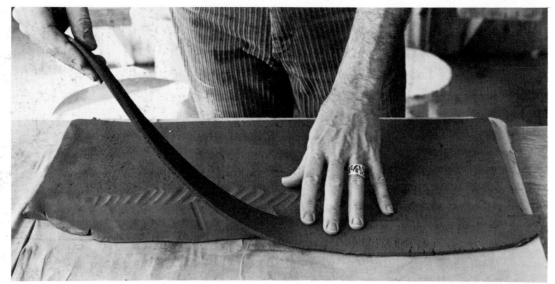

202

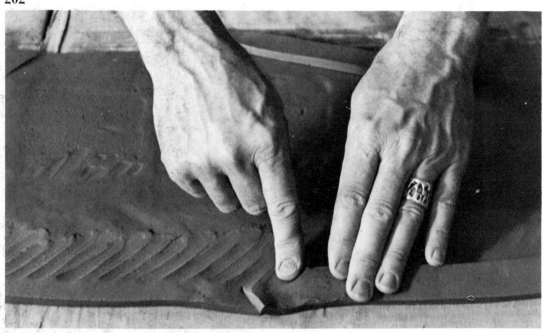

203

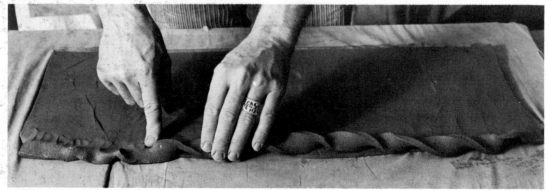

204

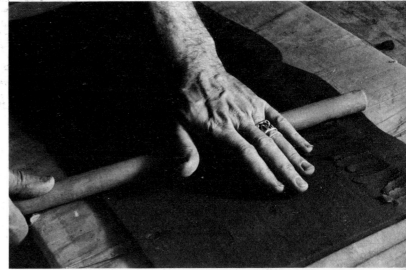

205

206

bottom and sides of the slab and re-attaches them in layers to what will be the top of the pot [202]. The strips may run the entire length of the slab [202] or may be attached in sections [203], either vertically or horizontally; he may also twist some strips before attaching them [204]. The strips overlap the main slab and are smoothed down and flattened with a dowel [205]. A window may be cut out in the center of the slab, and a small textured slab added face down. It is also smoothed down and rolled [206]. The texture on the small slabs is made by impressing weathered pieces of wood, nutshells, or any other interesting material into them, and it is given some definition by incising [207].

This usually completes the preparation of the slab. It is important to note that the slab, despite overlapping strips of clay, is perfectly uniform in thickness, since all overlaps have been rolled flat.

To form the pot the whole slab is folded

207

208

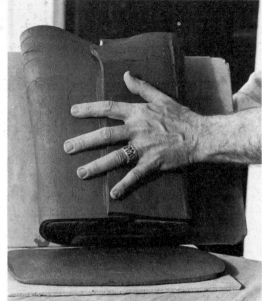

209

around a block of foam rubber [208], picked up with the aid of a board [209], and attached to a bottom. Miraculously, the attached strips of clay have resulted in a series of flowing lines, and the textured area seems to come from behind in a most subtle manner.

The overlap that has resulted from joining the slab is pulled up to form a freely sculptured unit on the inside of what might be considered the back of the pot [210]. This loosely formed unit is in contrast to the subtlety of the undulating lines and draws attention to the inside of the form.

To further emphasize the lines and add another dimension to the form, the upper part of the pot is pushed out gently from the inside. This stretches the clay and emphasizes the lines by opening them up [211]. Shames is able to do this because he completes the pot with the clay at the plastic stage.

Shames uses glazes very sparingly, leaving the textured areas unglazed, in order to avoid covering up the subtleties of the surface. He fires his work to stoneware temperatures in a reducing atmosphere.

210

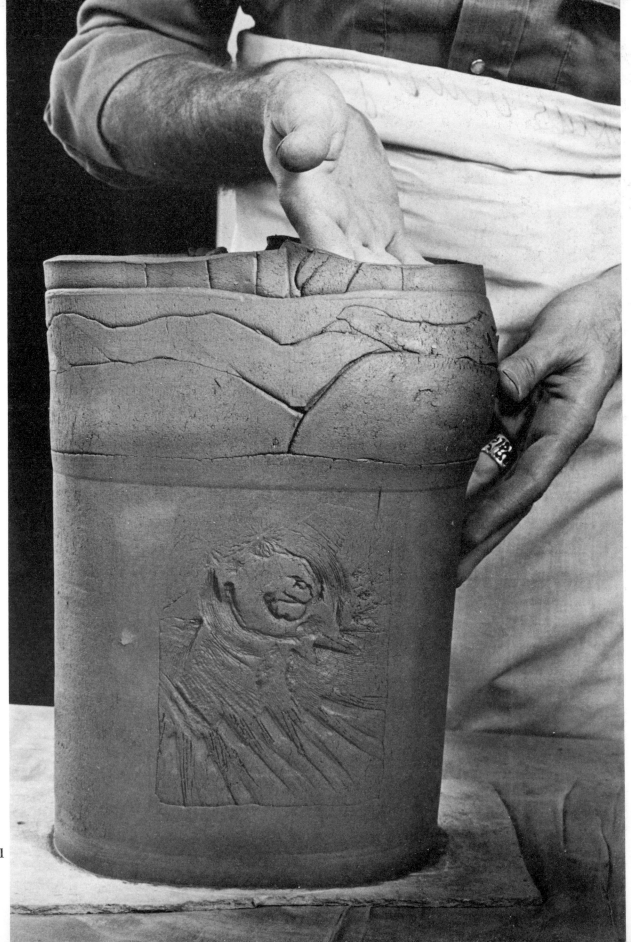

211

Billie Walters, raku form. 9" × 7"

BILLIE WALTERS

Billie Walters's bulbous swelling forms with their soft folds on top in no way give a clue as to the technique she uses. The forms seem too alive and pulsating to be, as they are, the result of the use of slabs with molds. Only a thorough understanding of the plastic nature of the clay would allow one to use these techniques with such remarkably fluid results.

To make half of her pot, Billie Walters lets a slab of plastic clay fall onto a plaster or bisque mold from the board on which she had pounded and rolled it out [212]. The slab is deliberately

212

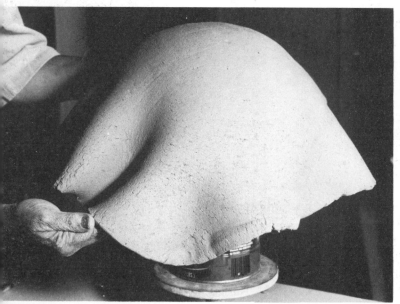

213

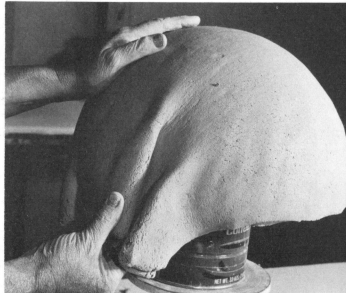

214

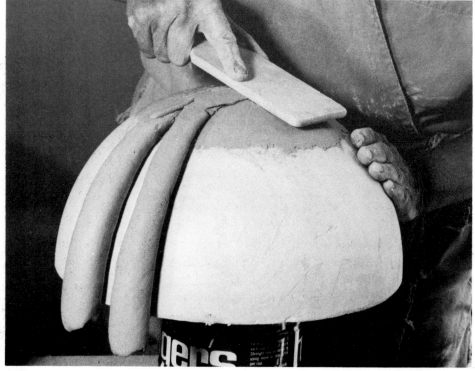

215

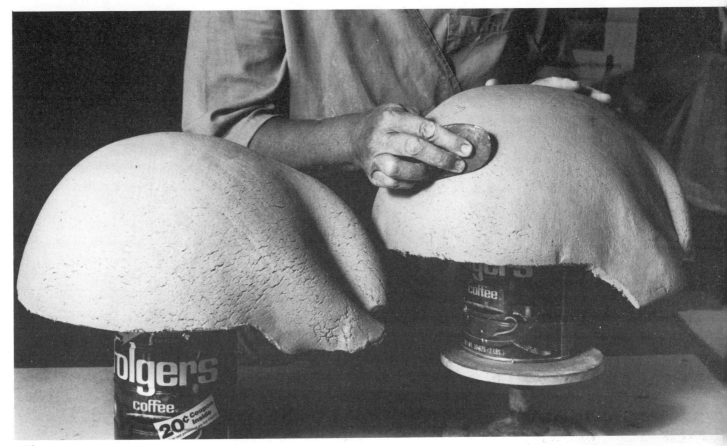

216

larger than needed, so that it drapes over the
mold in loose folds [213]. This is exactly what
she wants, since these folds will form the top of
her pots. She carefully chooses the correct fold
and may in some cases change its shape gently
[214]. To achieve variations in form, Walters
alters the form of the mold by adding clay to the
top or on the side in thick coils [215]. Except for
the fold, the excess of the clay slab is cut off along
the bottom edge of the mold. Walters makes
two such forms, one with slightly smaller folds
[216].

The clay forms are allowed to become leather-
hard on the mold. In the dry climate of New
Mexico, this takes only one or two hours. With
the smaller folds tucking under the larger ones,
the two forms are joined very carefully (scoring,
slipping, reinforcing with clay and paddling),
one side lying on a pillow to avoid denting [217].

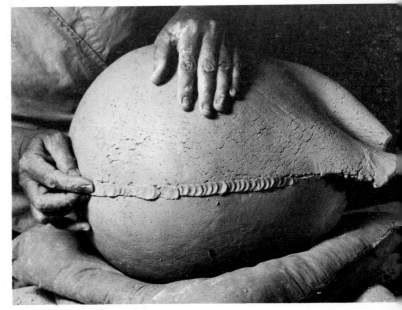

217

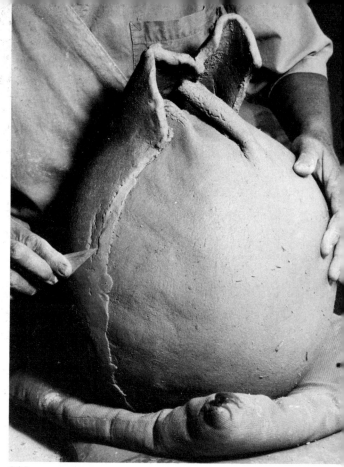

218

After the joining, the pot is placed in its proper vertical position on two pillows, so that the top can be sculpted [218].

The larger fold is paddled down over the smaller one [219], and the gaps are filled with clay [220]. Some of the seams may be obscured that way, while others are retained. Some of the pockets that are formed may be either exaggerated or diminished. It is at this point that Walters carefully considers all the details of the top in relation to each other and the whole pot. The folds and ridges are to grow out of the pot and give the appearance that they are the result of a force from the inside. They are the culmination of the whole piece, not a decoration or added appendage. The position and character of the opening is crucial [221]. It is the key to the force inside. It draws in and it also lets the inside escape.

As a final step, Walters eliminates all traces of the joint of the molded forms with a Surform tool and in some cases may even sandpaper the bone-dry clay. She is careful, though, to enhance the texture rather than obliterate it and to retain some of the cracks and stretch marks of the clay that are the result of the forming process [222].

Walters rarely uses glazes, but sponges on an engobe and may sometimes rub stains into it.

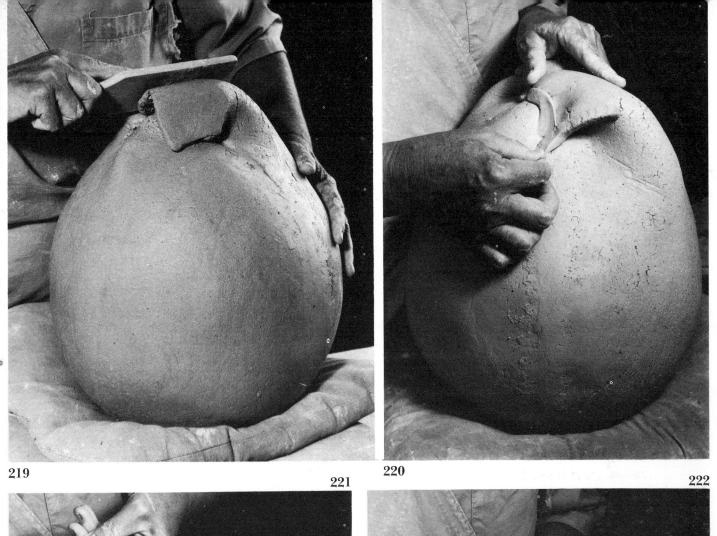

219

220

221

222

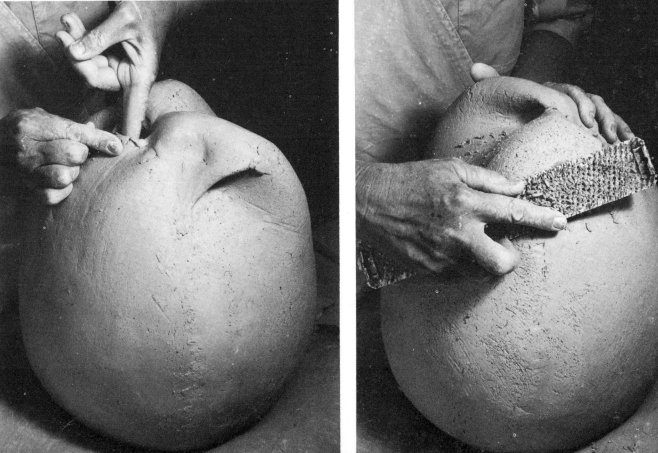

Susan Wechsler, raku container. 5″ × 14″

Susan Wechsler, Smoked Vessel. Raku. 12.5″ × 15″

Jeff Smith

SUSAN WECHSLER

Susan Wechsler's work is characterized by clean geometric lines, a sense of proportion, and an interest in the relationship of parts that is very much akin to that of an architect. This, according to her, is probably the result of living and working in an urban environment. At the same time, the work is by no means mechanical, since the plastic quality of the clay is neither ignored nor compromised.

Her work consists primarily of elliptical, hemispherical, and tubular forms. Sometimes she combines these forms, and she very often contrasts smooth and textured surfaces. Her work is done mostly with slabs, formed with the aid of a slab roller [223]. Wechsler is fascinated not only by the ease of making slabs in this manner but also by the perfection and strength of the slabs. For the elliptical forms, she presses the

223

224

225

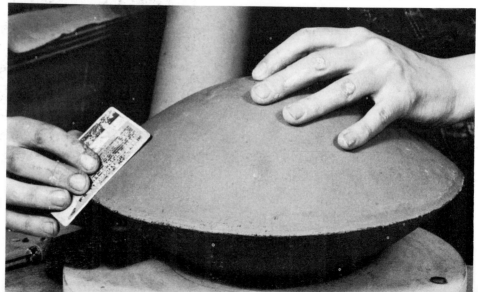

226

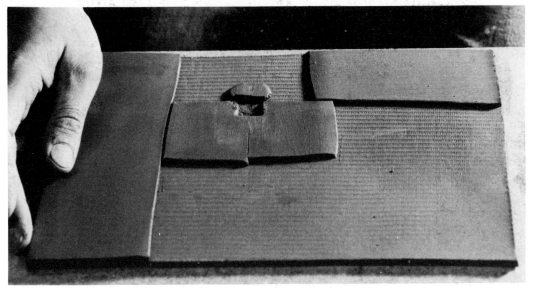

227

slab into a press mold by gently stretching the slab with a sponge [224]. At the leather-hard stage, two of these forms are joined. Before the joining, Wechsler carefully bevels the rim of the form to get as large a contact area as possible [225]. The seam is worked on with a credit card, which makes an excellent tool for smoothing the edge [226].

The tubular forms are made freehand from one slab. The texture and design are added before the form is made, with the slab flat on the table [227]. First, Wechsler textures the slab by impressing corduroy on it. Then very thin slabs are added on top of it in a geometric pattern. When these pieces are rolled onto the main slab with a huge rolling pin, they are not only joined firmly to the slab but also slightly altered in size and shape. To further relieve the severity of the forms and design, and to add another dimension, Wechsler likes to interrupt the pattern by pushing clay in a small area up into a ridge and flattening this ridge with a small roller.

When the slab is formed into a tube, the design changes again [228]. The shapes of the applied pieces of clay are distorted in ever so subtle a manner, and the spaces between them widen. These subtle changes stem from the plasticity of

228

the clay and are, in my opinion, the key to the vitality of Wechsler's work. This coupling of her love for geometric shapes and architectural designs with the flexibility and the responsiveness of clay results in vibrating works with cool, clean lines.

When joining the tubular form to an elliptical one, Wechsler cuts out the center of the elliptical form and joins the pieces together on the inside only [229].

Her elliptical forms with covers are made in a very similar fashion. A slab with a design applied to it [230] is pushed into a mold, with the design facing down. Again, Wechsler counts on the design's changing when the slab is pushed into the mold. At the leather-hard stage, it is joined to a similarly molded, plain form. A cover is cut out following the pattern of the applied pieces, and a slab relating to the shape of the applied piece of clay is added as a handle [231]. The cut is made at an angle, so that the beveled cut acts as a seat for the cover.

The character of Wechsler's forms reflects her method of working. She carefully plans the structure of each piece, sometimes arriving at the size of the slabs with the aid of a mathematical formula. She keeps careful record of the measurements, and the pieces of slabs are carefully

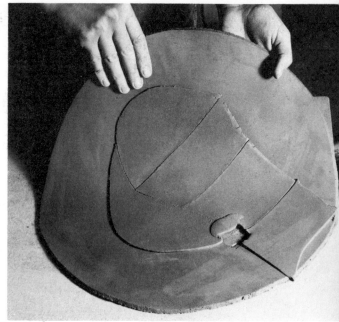

230

measured and drawn before they are cut out. The resulting forms could very easily be mechanical and stiff. Wechsler avoids this by balancing her structured approach with a high regard for the basic nature of clay; namely, its plasticity. And the fact that Wechsler raku or sawdust fires her work gives it another dimension of fluidity and daring.

231

229

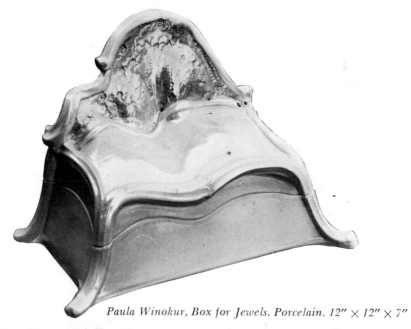

Paula Winokur, Box for Jewels. Porcelain. 12″ × 12″ × 7″

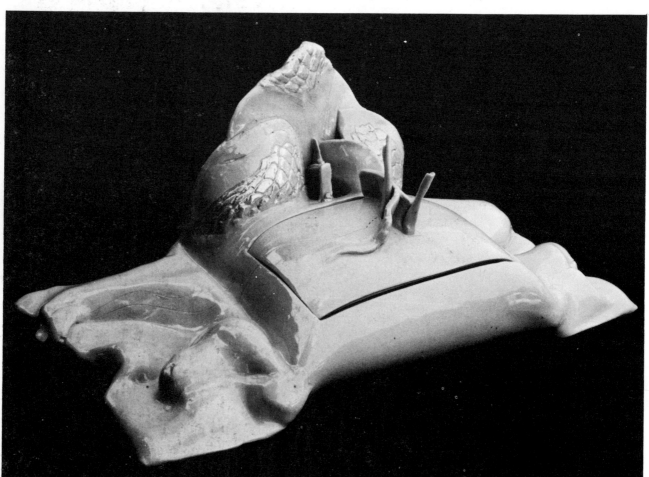

Paula Winokur, White Landscape. Double porcelain box. 10″ × 14″ × 7″

194

PAULA WINOKUR

Paula Winokur combines in all her work functional concerns with sculptural forms. In her sculptured container forms, this blend is particularly successful. The container gives the sculpture its volume and thereby its raison d'être, and the sculptural aspects of the form give the container its spirit and magic, while the porcelain adds a feeling of preciousness and a touch of the sensuous.

From the technical standpoint, the boxes and containers are the result of a complex combination of techniques. Paula Winokur uses a variety of methods. The forms may be slab-built or extruded, and in some instances she combines these two particular techniques. The process of making the forms consists of three distinct phases: preparing the parts [232–238]; assembling them [239–242]; and refining and enriching the form and surface [243, 244].

232

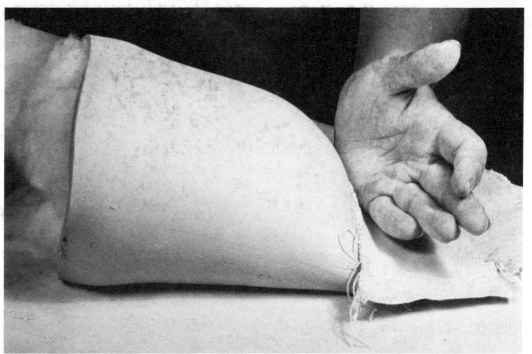

233

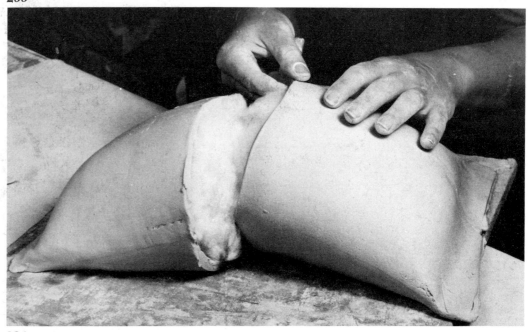

234

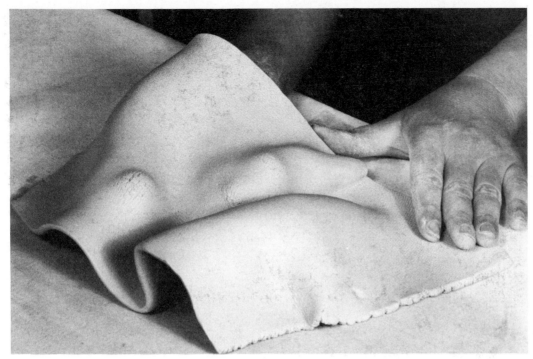

235

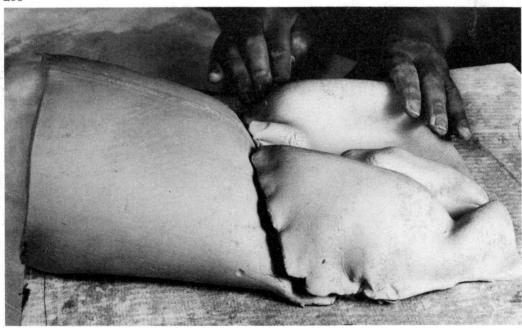

236

For the particular piece illustrated here, Winokur extruded two short cylinders for the containers [232], which were pinched together at one end and filled with Dacron [233, 234] so that they kept their shape until they were leather-hard. Slabs were undulated for the side sections by gathering and pushing up from underneath [235]. Their form was then adjusted to the extruded parts [236]. The surface of the slabs for the vertical part was impressed with

237

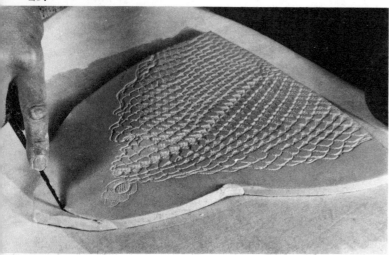

238

239

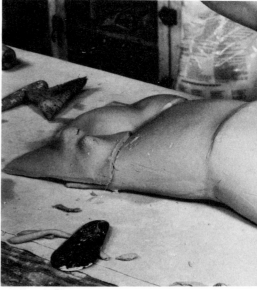

241

lace [**237, 238**]. (Every slab was made on a slab roller.)

All parts were allowed to dry to the leather-hard stage, at which time they were assembled. One of the extruded parts was closed off with a slab and the other attached to it [**239, 240**]. This interior slab acts both as a vertical support that keeps the tubes from flattening out and as a means to give the container two separate compartments. The side sections [**241**] as well as the vertical section were then attached to the extruded parts and worked into the form [**242**]. For structural strength, and to give a feeling of volume, the vertical part always consists of a double-walled piece or a shallow box built from leather-hard slabs.

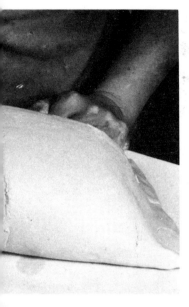

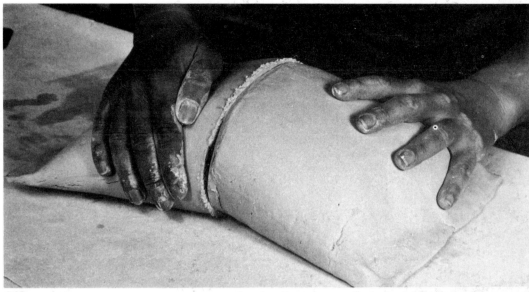

240

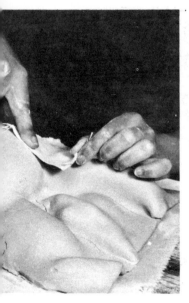

242

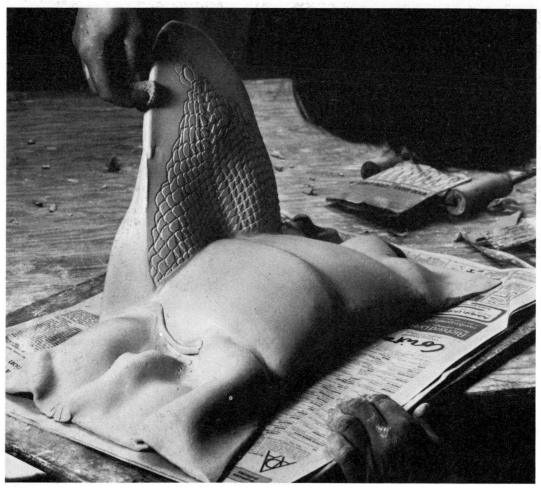

243

In assembling, Winokur scores the clay and applies water liberally. Clay coils, usually dipped in water, are used for reinforcements and to fill gaps. It is interesting that Winokur does not paddle the joints or the forms, but prefers to rub them, always with a cloth between the clay and her hand or finger [233, 241].

Throughout the process of assembling, Winokur adjusts the forms to each other, concerning herself with the flow of the forms and their relationship. Elements of her environment—the softly rolling landscape of eastern Pennsylvania—appear in most of her work.

After assembling, a great deal of time is spent on enriching the surface of the form by adding clay in coils or dots, by drawing, and by refining the edges [243]. This surface enrichment, however, is never allowed to remain on the surface; it becomes part of the form by defining and emphasizing it. It is this surface enrichment and its relationship to the form that characterize all of Winokur's work. It is at this point that Paula Winokur exploits the characteristics of porcelain. Its smooth surface both brings out and contrasts with every facet and detail of the surface enrichment.

Since Winokur always completes the form as a totally closed unit, the last step is to open up the container by cutting the covers out of the extruded parts. The outline of the covers was es-

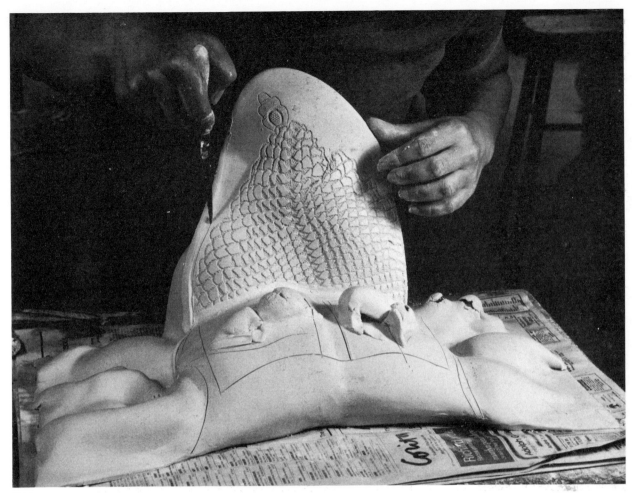

244

tablished in the previous surface-enrichment phase as part of the line drawings and the knobs as part of the sculptural forms [**244**].

In this complex procedure of making a piece, the artist exploits the plasticity of the clay on the one hand, and the structural strength of leather-hard clay on the other. The former allows the artist to achieve rich undulating forms, while the latter helps her combine them into a highly complex arrangement of forms.

The other important aspect of her pieces is the integration of sculptural forms and surface treatment into a piece containing elements of landscape and displaying a baroque richness of detail.

Elsbeth S. Woody, Long L's I. Unglazed stoneware. 5' × 10' × 4'

ELSBETH S. WOODY

In an effort to overcome the limitations of my kiln and build environmental pieces, I developed a system of working with multiples. I found that if the individual unit is kept very simple, it is the interaction between the units that creates the form; the total, then, is different from the sum of its parts.

The idea of using multiples is obviously not new, but to my knowledge it is rarely used with clay, unless the units are made with molds. Initially, I made each unit individually because of a lack of familiarity with molds, and the fact that not all the pieces were exactly the same size. I do so now out of conviction, since the slight variations in the forms give my pieces an organic feeling I find missing in sculptures that use the principle of multiples but have them produced by an industrial process.

The formation of the units is relatively easy. At present I am interested in oval tubular forms that are built using the extended pinch method. I will discuss the techniques used to build two variations of this oval tubular form—the L-shape and the loop.

For the L-shape, I use what I call the *purzelbaum,* or somersault method, which means that each piece goes through three stages, in the process of which the piece is flipped twice. In stage one, a cylinder plus the start of the curve is built standing upright [245]. In stage two, this cylin-

245

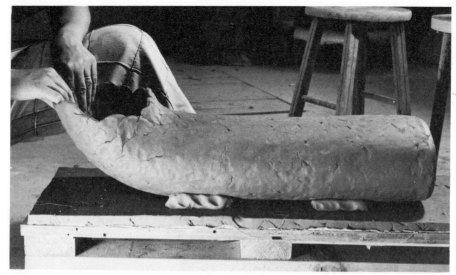

246

247

der is laid down with the curve pointing up [246], and the rest of the curve, plus what will be the horizontal arm of the L, is formed in a vertical position [247]. In stage three, another flip occurs to put the just-finished part in its proper horizontal position [248]. The cylinder that was built in stage one is now again vertical but upside down [249]. This part is cut off and replaced

248

249

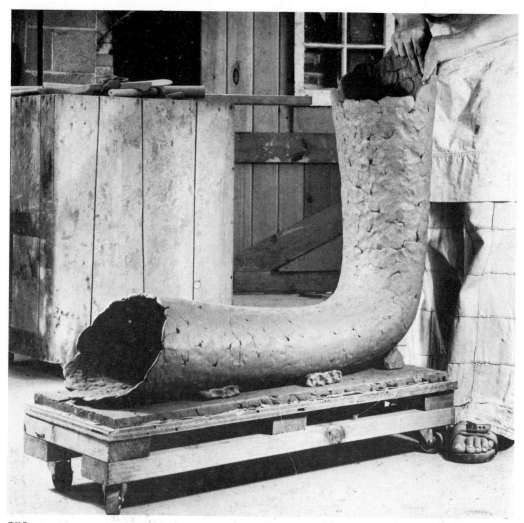

250

with a newly pinched section [250]. This double flip is necessary because neither end is flat.

Let me outline the details for making L-shapes. In stage one, the height of the cylinder depends on the length of the horizontal arm of the finished L-shape. The longer the arm is, the longer the cylinder needs to be, in order to counterbalance it in stage two. For the same reason, I make it deliberately heavy. I would not make the cylinder any less than two-thirds the length of the horizontal arm.

In stage two, the piece is laid down after it has been allowed to get thoroughly leather-hard (except for the curved part). The curve is then completed in several stages, and what will be-

come the horizontal arm is completed in an upright position. While one builds the vertical part, the curve has to be supported with clay [247]. The curve must be leather-hard, or the support will dent it. I frequently use a level to make sure that the arm is truly vertical [251].

Rather than striving for a perfect tube, I like to make the arms of the L slightly trumpet-shaped by slowly increasing the diameter. I also compensate for the slight flattening out that occurs in the firing by increasing the diameter in the other direction. For the same reason, I attach semicircular discs on the curve for supports, spaced every 5″ to 8″ [252].

In stage three, one has to be very careful when

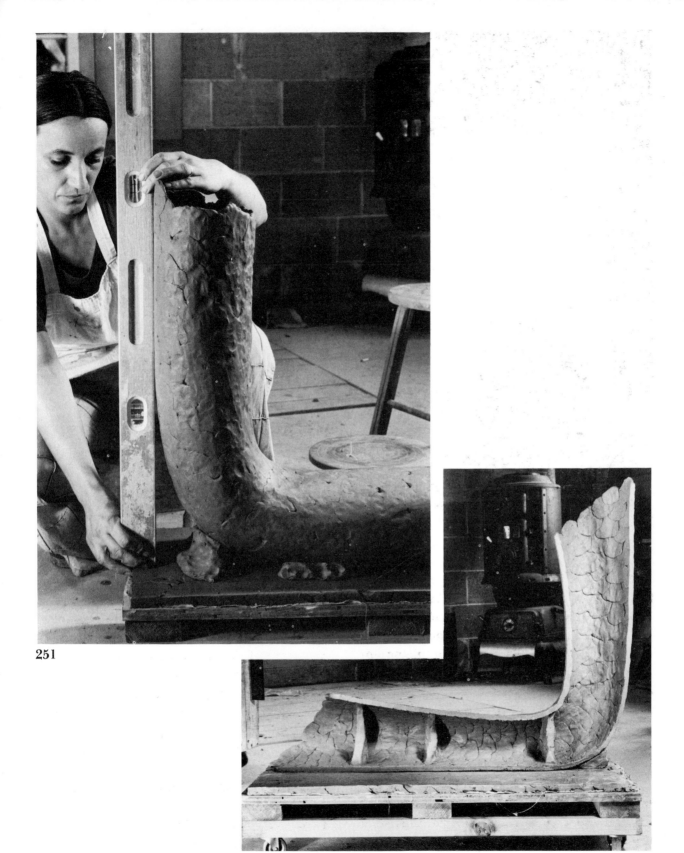

251

252

253

flipping the piece (after it has become leather-hard, of course). I make sure that my clay supports are within reach [248] and, whenever possible, ask someone to help me. After the flipping, the now vertical part (which is the cylinder that was built in stage one) is cut off just above the curve [249]. I do this for several reasons: because I pinched it heavier, so that it would counterbalance the other arm; because it has usually lost its shape somewhat and is too hard to be adjusted; because there is too much of a discrepancy in the consistency of the clay between the rim, which was the very bottom of the first cylinder, and the plastic clay that would be added to make the point; because it allows me to resoften the curved part so that I can adjust its shape; and because I can add a support on the inside of the tube just within the curve if I intend to make the

vertical arm very high [252]. Again, I frequently check the angle of the arm with a level.

The second variation of the oval tubular form is the loop shape. The loops [253] are built by placing two columns [254] the proper distance apart on the clay slab. I work in from either side, using a Masonite template. The template, however, serves only as a general guide [255]. Since I have to work in numerous stages at this point, the relationship to the guide changes as the clay shrinks. When the two sides meet, I weave them together by overlapping the pinch on top on one side and tucking it under on the other [256]. With the next pinch, I reverse this procedure. In addition, I deliberately create a slight upward bulge at this point, both to allow for the shrinkage and to avoid an indentation or a flat place in

254

255

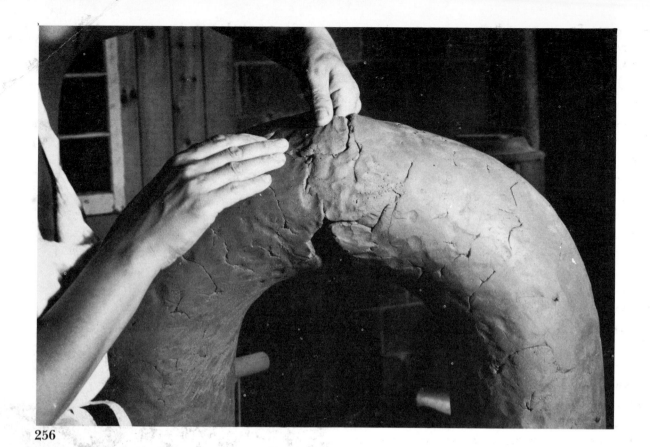

256

Elsbeth S. Woody, Short L's II. Unglazed stoneware. 2′ × 7′ × 10′

the curve. The upward bulge is easily paddled down at the leather-hard stage.

The loop with the horizontal extension [253] is built by combining an L-shaped form with the loop. Build one straight cylinder and an L-shape, then place them in the same manner that you would place the two vertical columns of the loop, and connect them.

I use the extended pinch method for all my forms and work in numerous stages, particularly around the curved sections. After completing each stage, I cover the top edge, and when that section is leather-hard, I refine the surface and form by paddling, before continuing.

Almost all the pieces are built on a clay slab, to make sure the supports stay right with them during shrinkage. The loops are also placed on a clay slab, so that the bottom of the columns are moved in as the top loop shrinks. The clay slab is placed on ¾″ thick plywood, and to avoid ever having to lift anything, I place everything on a dolly [253].

When one is working on a large scale, proper planning is essential. I make models with clay coils to work out my ideas, and derive the approximate proportions from the clay model. The exact dimensions are then figured out on paper. The dollies and plywood bases are cut to fit each form exactly. This allows me to place the pieces in their intended position in relation to each other without removing them from the dolly [253].

Careful measuring, working with a level, and at times the use of a template make it possible to duplicate forms fairly precisely. However, what seems almost more important is to make same-size pieces at the same time, instead of one after another. One falls into a rhythm that almost eliminates measuring.

Once all the pieces are finished and dried, they are placed in the kiln on the wooden boards. The fact that I have a car kiln, with the car coming into a ditch into my studio, greatly facilitates the stacking of the kiln [257].

Only two inches of the boards burns away. The rest turns to charcoal because of a lack of air underneath the clay slab. This is why no movement takes place, and there is no danger of a tall piece tipping over.

Installation is another step in making large-scale work; not only the safety of the piece but also the safety of the viewer has to be considered. The needs are different for each type of installation, either outdoor or indoor. In either case, I make sure that each tube has a pipe inside that will keep it from falling over. Outside, the pipe is anchored in the ground, and for installation in shows, it is bolted to the base.

257

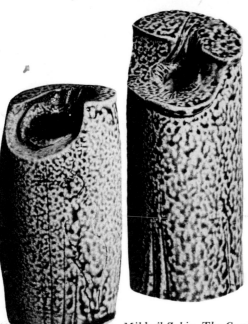

Mikhail Zakin, The Couple. Salt glazed. 13″ × 6″ × 6″, 14.5″ × 6″ × 6″

Mikhail Zakin, Metamorphic Form. Salt glazed. 6″ × 5″ × 10″

MIKHAIL ZAKIN

Mikhail Zakin's primary interest is (to use her own words) "the articulated clay form that reveals its structure." Her pieces are expressions of metamorphosis—forms in the process of change. She prefers to salt-glaze or carbonize her pieces, since these processes most clearly reveal the underlying form.

Her concern is not with methodology—she is interested in eliciting different responses from clay and in observing the emergence of forms as she works with the material, exploring its plasticity. This conceptual approach is coupled with an almost scientific approach to problem solving.

She gives herself a set of conditions from which she starts an experiment, using a combination of traditional and not-so-traditional techniques. For instance, she may pierce a solid block of clay with a two-by-four [258], stretch the clay by

258

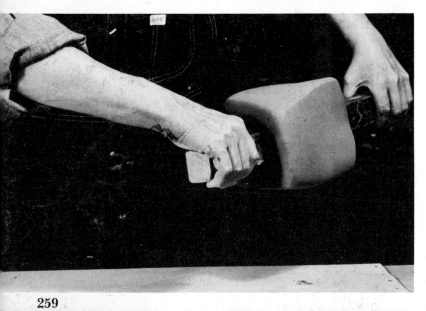

259

260

261

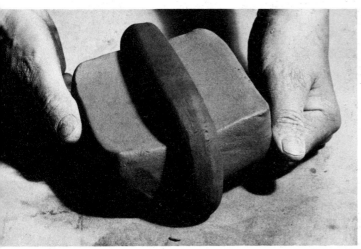

262

263

264

throwing it, with the stick in it, sideways on the table [259], and hit it with a sharp-edged board [260]. The result is a beautiful form with freely flowing sides and a forceful texture [261].

Or a thick package of light-colored clay is surrounded with a coil of darker clay [262] and stretched out over a hump mold [263]. This time, there emerges an angular form with a beautiful curve on the inside and a rim that speaks of the plasticity of the clay. The dark coil becomes a band that traverses the bowl and turns into protrusions [264].

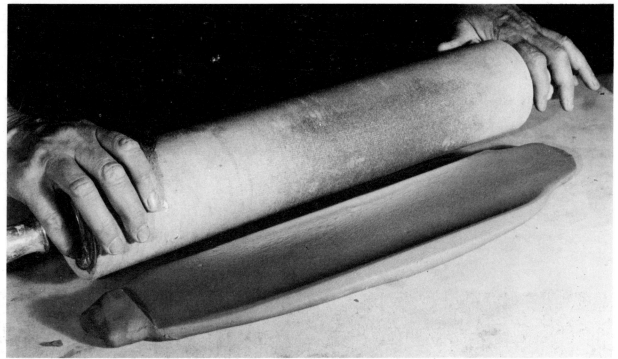

265

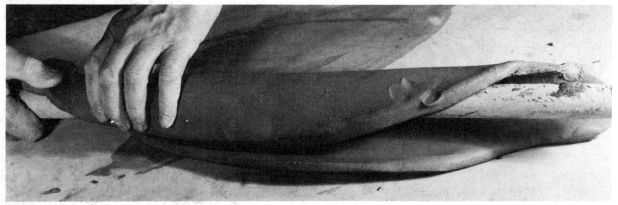

266

Another time, a thick coil is turned into a long, narrow slab with a ridge (made with the aid of a rolling pin) running lengthwise down its center [265]. The slab is turned into a tube [266] and bent [267]. The spine compresses while the skin stretches.

Mikhail Zakin's approach stands out not only in conceptual terms but also by virtue of the techniques used. While not shunning traditional methods, Zakin either adapts existing techniques or more importantly, unencumbered by do's and don'ts, regularly experiments with clay to find new ways to express her imagery. The common denominator of her work is her concern for expressive form and for the development of these forms through constant "dialogue" with the plastic clay.

267

Conclusion

Numerous factors influence any creative endeavor. An appropriate question to ask here is how and to what extent techniques influence one's work. The answer differs from artist to artist and may be different at various points in time. For some, technique comes first and the concept grows out of it; for others, the choice of technique is determined by the concept.

Each technique brings with it both limitations and possibilities. Each artist deals with the limitations differently and exploits the possibilities in his or her own way. The choices we make in terms of techniques, their limitations and possibilities, determine our approach or are determined by it.

A piece, therefore, stands at a point where one's choice of techniques, one's goals and conceptual concerns, as well as one's aesthetic persuasion, come together.

This is the reason for the diversity of forms in ceramic art. It also defines the challenge for the mature ceramicist as well as the newcomer: to integrate conceptual approach with choice of technique into a work that expresses one's concerns.

Appendix
Clay-Body and Glaze Recipes
Used by the Artists

The following are the clay body and glaze recipes used by the artists featured in "Ten Approaches to Handbuilding." Be careful to note the maturing temperatures of the clay and glazes, and, as with any recipe, test them before applying to your favorite piece.

ELAINE KATZER

STONEWARE CLAY BODY: cone 6

Lincoln Fire Clay	7–10
Pacific Sewer Pipe Clay	7–10
Grog IONE Grain Interpace #409	3.5
Agrashell 30 mesh	1.5

Agrashell is ground walnut shells and is, to my knowledge, only available in Los Angeles.

WHITE ENGOBE:

EPK Kaolin	25
Ball Clay	25
Kingman Feldspar	25
Flint	25

For blue, add 2 percent Cobalt Oxide.

Katzer uses Iron Chromate mixed with water and brushed on the greenware for black, and for yellow, Rutile mixed with water.

ELIZABETH MACDONALD

CLAY BODY:

MacDonald uses a clay called Sandstone Buff from California.

GLAZE:

Leach Temoku: cone 8 Oxidation

Potash Feldspar	544
Whiting	462
EPK Kaolin	136
Flint	658
Red Iron Oxide	211

DAVID MIDDLEBROOK

CLAY BODIES:

Common Whiteware: cone 06

Ball Clay	50
Talc	40
Plastic Vitrox	10
Sand 30 mesh (optional)	10

Sculpture Mix: cone 06

Lincoln Sixty	60
Tennessee Ball Clay	40
Talc	25
Mixed Sand (20 and 30 mesh)	10
Mixed Grog (20 and 30 mesh)	10

White Stoneware: cone 6

Lincoln Sixty	25
Tennessee Ball Clay	25
EPK Kaolin	25
Talc	25
Sand	10

GLAZES:

For brightly colored glazes (particularly reds, yellows, and oranges) with matte and dry surface textures, Middlebrook usually uses commercial underglazes either on top of or underneath other glazes. Some examples:

First coat: a mixture of any low-fire matte glaze and ball clay in equal parts, ball-milled and sprayed on in a thin layer.

Second coat: commercial underglaze, sprayed or brushed on.

Or:

First coat: commercial underglaze.

Second coat: any matte glaze sprayed on in a thin layer.

Slightly underfire for a truly matte finish.

Or:

First coat: Middlebrook's Cactus Red Glaze (see below).

Second coat: commercial underglaze, thin application.

The following glazes can be used in conjunction with each other or with Middlebrook's Cactus Red. Variations in thickness of application, and firing in a reducing or oxidizing atmosphere, result in a wide range of colors.

Orange Green: cone 06

White Lead	83.3
Kaolin	30
Flint	16
Potassium Dichromate	10
Tin (or Zircopax)	5 (10)

Desert Red: cone 06

White Lead	92
Soda Feldspar	11
Barium Carbonate	4
Flint	5
Chrome Oxide	6

Not-Mellon-Yellow: cone 06

White Lead	500
Bentonite	25
Flint	25

Magnesium Zirconium Silicate	100
Soda Ash	150
Potassium Dichromate	25

Middlebrook's Cactus Red: cone 06

White Lead	120
Silica	7
Kingman Feldspar	14
Barium Carbonate	5
Chrome Oxide	7.5

For a cracked effect, use:

First coat: any matte, satin, or glossy glaze of your choice of color.

Second coat: kiln wash or Duncan's Bark Glaze or slip, in a thick coat.

Third coat: commercial underglaze, sprayed on.

The color of the third coat is the color of the overall surface, with the color of the first coat coming through in the crackles.

It is important to note that the brilliant colors in Middlebrook's work are due in part to the fact that he works with a white clay. In addition, prior to glazing, he sometimes applies metallic oxides (red-oranges: Iron; blues: Cobalt; greens: Chrome, Iron; yellows: Iron, Rutile) directly on the bisque and sponges off the excess. This helps to bring out the textures of the pieces and works well in transitions from one area to the other.

DONNA NICHOLAS

EARTHENWARE CLAY BODY:

Cedar Heights Stoneware	40
Ball Clay	30
EPK Kaolin	10
Talc	10
Sand	10
Bentonite	2

GLAZES:

Alkaline Base Glaze

Frit 3110	22
Potash Feldspar	10.85
Barium Carbonate	5.5
EPK Kaolin	7
Cornwall Stone	5

Add 10% Zircopax for more whiteness.

Cone 06 oxidation in gas kiln; cone 05 in electric kiln.

White Lead Base

White Lead	64
Potash Feldspar	19.4
Barium Carbonate	9
EPK Kaolin	3.8
Cornwall Stone	3.8

This glaze is used for orange and yellow colors.

Add 5% Rutile for a warm tan;

2–8% Potassium D-Chromate for yellow to red-orange;

4–8% Nickel for gray-green;

½% Cobalt Oxide + 4% Nickel for green.

Nicholas also uses Hommel's Powdered Underglazes and Hommel's Glaze Stains mixed in with the glazes at about 10% for different colors.

SY SHAMES

STONEWARE CLAY BODY: cone 7

Jordan	8
Missouri Fire Clay	6
PBX AP Green	6
Grog	1

GLAZE BASE:

Potash Feldspar	38
Frit 3417	27
Dolomite	9
Whiting	11.5
Kaolin	25

BILLIE WALTERS

RAKU CLAY BODY (Variation of Paul Soldner):

Lincoln Fire Clay	50
Talc	20
Grog or Sand	30

ENGOBE:

Gerstley Borate	100
Kaolin	100
Silica	100

Engobe is sponged on about the thickness of a normal glaze application.

STAIN (over Engobe):

Red Iron Oxide	10
Copper Carbonate	5
Borax	Some

SUSAN WECHSLER

RAKU CLAY BODY:

Fire Clay	50
Bonding Clay	20
Ball Clay	30
Talc	10
Wollastonite (C-6)	10
Mullite, 35 mesh	15
Grog	10

RAKU GLAZES:

Soldner's Clear

Gerstley Borate	80
Nepheline Syenite	20

Soldner's Glassy Red

Gerstley Borate	80
Borax	50
Red Iron Oxide	10
Copper Oxide	5

Piepenberg's Copper Cobalt

Colemanite	80
Cornwall Stone	20
Cobalt Carbonate	¼
Copper	2

Zimmerman's Copper

Frit 3134	45
Gerstley Borate	40
Flint	7
Kaolin	8

PAULA WINOKUR

PORCELAIN BODY: cone 10 Reduction

Grolleg Clay	55
Flint	15
Feldspar (Potash)	20
Wollastonite or Pyrophyllite	5
Molochite Grog 100 mesh	5
Bentonite	4

TRANSPARENT GLAZE: cone 10 Reduction

Buckingham Spar	28.5
Ball Clay	19.5
Whiting	19.5
Silica	32.5

Red Iron Oxide 1 percent for Celadon.

BLUISH WHITE GLAZE: cone 10 Reduction

Buckingham Spar	37.4

Whiting	14.7
Ash (Wood, very fine)	4.5
China Clay	13.1
Flint	27.4
Colemanite	2.9

For Celadon, add 1 percent Red Iron Oxide. Sieve several times through a 100-mesh screen.

ELSBETH S. WOODY

STONEWARE CLAY BODY: cone 8 Reduction

Jordan	35
Missouri Fire Clay	35
Flint	10
Ohio Red Clay	10
Grog	15

MIKHAIL ZAKIN

CLAY BODY FOR SALT GLAZING: cone 10

Jordan 50	50
Missouri Fire Clay	50
Ball Clay	25
F4 Feldspar	5
Sand	10
Bentonite	1.5

Glossary

BISQUE—the firing in preparation for glazing in which the temperature is brought up to a point just before vitrification

BONE-DRY—completely air-dried

BUTT JOINT—a joint where the end of a slab butts against another slab or the end of a slab. Coils also butt on top of each other

CONE—a small pyramidal form commercially made from ceramic materials and used to measure the heat in the kiln

EARTHENWARE—all ceramic ware that fires below 1800° F.

ENGOBE—a type of slip made from various colored clays and used to paint the surface of ceramic forms

GLAZE—a compound of minerals that forms a glassy coating on ceramic ware when subjected to sufficient heat

GREENWARE—all ceramic ware prior to firing

GROG—fired clay ground to various mesh sizes

KILN—enclosed containers of various sizes—built of refractory brick and heated by electricity, gas, oil, or wood to temperatures from 1500° to 2300° F.—in which pots are fired

LEATHER-HARD—stage of the clay between plastic and bone-dry

MATURING POINT—the point in firing when the clay has vitrified enough to be hard and durable and a glaze melts

MINERAL—earthy substance with a definite chemical formula

OVERLAP JOINT—a joint where two pieces of clay overlap each other

OXIDATION FIRING—the method of firing in which complete combustion takes place, or the type of firing that results from the use of an electric kiln

PLASTIC CLAY—the consistency of clay when it is dry enough not to stick to one's hands but wet enough for a coil to bend without cracking

PORCELAIN—all ceramic ware made of a white clay and fire above 2300° F.

RAKU—the method of firing in which the pot is put into a red-hot kiln, withdrawn as soon as the glaze melts, and then carbonized (smoked) by putting it into a closed container of easily combustible material, such as sawdust or pine needles. The whole firing cycle may take less than half an hour, and raku firings usually reach temperatures of earthenware

REDUCTION FIRING—the method of firing in which the incomplete combustion of the fuel produces free carbon monoxide, which in turn strips the metallic oxides in the clay and glazes of oxygen

REFRACTORY—resistant to melting

REPROCESSING—reclaiming clay that is either too wet or too dry to be worked with, by soaking it in water until it breaks up and then pouring it on plaster slabs to dry to the proper consistency for reuse

SALT GLAZING—the method of firing in which salt is introduced into the hot kiln. The vapors of the burning salt combine with the silica in the clay to form a glaze on the surface of the pot. Ware that is salt-glazed classifies as stoneware

SAWDUST FIRING—the method of firing in which the pot is placed into a container (metal drum) filled with sawdust. The sawdust is lit and the pot is fired by the heat produced by the slowly burning sawdust. Temperatures reached in such a manner range from 1000° to 1500° F., and the ware comes out thoroughly carbonized

SLIP—clay at a mayonnaise consistency

STAINS—metallic oxides mixed with water, used to change the color of a clay

STONEWARE—all ceramic ware fired between 2100° and 2300° F.

TRIMMING TOOL—a tool, with wire loops at both ends, that can be used to carve clay

VITRIFICATION—the melting of certain clay components and the forming of a glassy structure within the clay

WATER OF PLASTICITY—water between the particles of clay

WEDGING—method of kneading clay to make it homogeneous

Bibliographical Note

Excellent sources of detailed information on clay, glazes, and firing techniques as they apply to the studio potter are Daniel Rhodes's *Clay and Glazes for the Potter; Stoneware and Porcelain;* as well as *Kilns: Design, Construction and Operation.* W. G. Lawrence's *Ceramic Science for the Potter* deals with the same subject matter, but from a more scientific point of view. It offers the technical explanations for many things potters have learned by experience.

A very useful source on the technology of clay, glazes, and firings is also F. H. Norton's *Fine Ceramics, Technology and Application,* even though it deals with these matters more in terms of commercially produced wares.

Excellent sources for various specific subjects are Jack Troy's *Salt-Glazed Ceramics,* Hal Rieggers's *Primitive Pottery* and *Raku,* as well as Christopher Tyler and Richard Hirsch's *Raku: Techniques for Contemporary Potters.*

C. F. Binns's *The Potter's Craft* and Bernard Leach's *A Potter's Book* are classic pottery books. They deal with a wide range of subjects, from ceramic history to forming methods, but are most interesting because of the very personal outlook of these historically important potters. Michael Cardew's *Pioneer Pottery* falls into the same category but also offers information on natural sources of clay and glazes.

Marguerite Wildenhain's *Pottery: Form and Expression* and *The Invisible Core* deal with the effect working with clay has on a person, and M. C. Richards's *Centering in Pottery, Poetry and the Person* creates a philosophy based on the principles of wheelthrowing.

Paulus Berensohn's *Finding One's Way with Clay* and Daniel Rhodes' *Pottery Forms* are good examples of works that combine philosophy with process.

For a look at contemporary ceramics, see Tony Birks's *Art of the Modern Potter* and Eileen Lewenstein and Emmanuel Cooper's *New Ceramics.*

PERIODICALS

Craft Horizons, American Crafts Council, 44 West 53rd Street, New York, New York, 10019

Ceramic Monthly, Box 12448, Columbus, Ohio, 43212

Studio Potter, Box 172, Warner, New Hampshire, 03278

8637

£6.50

12.12.79